Sisterhood Heals

"*Sisterhood Heals* is full of guidance and insights on building and nurturing solid relationships with other women. The book provides practical advice for developing new friendships, enhancing existing ones, and examining one's own behavior in relationships. Dr. Joy Harden Bradford offers a roadmap for personal growth and improved connections with others, ultimately leading to a more fulfilling and joyful life. This is a valuable resource for anyone seeking to deepen their relationships with other women and cultivate a sense of sisterhood."

—NEDRA GLOVER TAWWAB, therapist and *New York Times* bestselling author of *Set Boundaries, Find Peace* and *Drama Free*

"*Sisterhood Heals* is a revelatory work about caring for ourselves and for our friends, and about how our relationships impact us in more ways than we ever realized. Inspiring, wise, and thoughtful, this book is a gift for anyone looking to deepen their friendships."

—LUVVIE AJAYI JONES, *New York Times* bestselling author of *Professional Troublemaker*

"Like many Black women, the bonds and sisterhood that I have with the women in my family and my own circle of sisters are some of the most valued and important in my life. *Sisterhood Heals* takes a deep dive into not just the beauty, but the science and the intricacies behind these relationships. It gives Black women and girls permission to celebrate our bonds, understand ourselves more deeply, mourn our losses, and find and maintain the community we need to heal. It is a gift."

—TARANA BURKE, *New York Times* bestselling author of *Unbound: My Story of Liberation and the Birth of the Me Too Movement*

"Dr. Joy's work joins a long legacy of Black women writing us into new realities of wellness and connection. *Sisterhood Heals* is an exceptional new text for us to learn from. It's a loving reminder that we are our sister's keeper and she is ours. If you want to feel seen and be lovingly invited to build life-changing relationships, read this book and share it with a friend."

—RACHEL E. CARGLE, author of *A Renaissance of Our Own*

"This book expands the potential for what is possible for each of us in relationship to others. For many, there is a collective wound around safety and support in friendship. As humans we long for connection but don't always have the tools to meet that need in a meaningful way. Dr. Joy's work continues to free people everywhere through her depth, expertise, authenticity, and courage to show the way forward in circumstances most don't share aloud."

—DEVI BROWN, founder, Devi Brown Well-Being

"As the only child of a single parent, my chosen family has been my saving grace. This book feels like an offering for the altars of their sisterhood, love, and guidance. And, most important, a skilled handbook on knowing how to preserve those connections."

—FRAN MEDINA, wellness advocate, producer, and founder of Hey Fran Hey

"[Dr. Joy] shines in her impressive debut, an exploration of the power of Black female friendship. Bradford's celebration of friendship is moving, backed with psychological depth, and especially welcome in a culture that sometimes downplays nonromantic bonds. This is food for the soul."

—*Publishers Weekly*

Sisterhood Heals

Sisterhood Heals

THE TRANSFORMATIVE POWER OF HEALING IN COMMUNITY

Joy Harden Bradford, PhD

BALLANTINE BOOKS
NEW YORK

2024 Ballantine Books Trade Paperback Edition

Published in the United States by Ballantine Books,
an imprint of Random House, a division of
Penguin Random House LLC, New York.

BALLANTINE BOOKS & colophon are registered trademarks
of Penguin Random House LLC.

Originally published in hardcover in the United States
by Ballantine Books, an imprint of Random House,
a division of Penguin Random House LLC, in 2023.

LIBRARY OF CONGRESS CATALOGING-IN-PUBLICATION DATA
Names: Bradford, Joy Harden, author.
Title: Sisterhood heals : the transformative power of healing in community /
Joy Harden Bradford, PhD.
Description: First edition. | New York : Ballantine Books, [2023] |
Includes bibliographical references.
Identifiers: LCCN 2023001241 (print) | LCCN 2023001242 (ebook) |
ISBN 9780593497265 (trade paperback) | ISBN 9780593497258 (ebook)
Subjects: LCSH: Female friendship—Psychological aspects. | African American
women—Social networks. | African American women—Social conditions. |
Healing circles.
Classification: LCC BF575.F66 B724 2023 (print)
LCC BF575.F66 (ebook)
DDC 158.2/5—dc23/eng/20230322
LC record available at https://lccn.loc.gov/2023001241
LC ebook record available at https://lccn.loc.gov/2023001242

Printed in the United States of America on acid-free paper

randomhousebooks.com

1st Printing

Book design by Alexis Flynn

To my sisters
May we always see one another

Contents

I sent my Baby to the window to buy ice cream on her own while I kept watch from the car directly across from where she was standing. Some guys came up next to her, greeted her politely, and stood patiently. One began engaging her in light conversation. I saw in her body language that she was getting nervous and was on my way to stand with her when this super fly Sista with a fade, sundress, and dragon wing tattooed backpiece came out of nowhere and said, "Heeeeeey, Little Sis! It's a good day for ice cream, huh?", then placed herself between my daughter and the guy.

All of Zoë's tension melted away. Supa Sista stayed with her until she got her cone and walked her back to my car where she winked at me before saying, "She did fine, Mama. We're all watching." She motioned over to her own car and there were four Sistas outside of it, all grinning and giving me the thumbs up.

I think that says a lot about how angels work. How the village works. How Black Women work.

We out here. Holy and fabulous and ready to ride out at any time, even at the ice cream shop.

—*Whitney Syphax Walker*, Facebook post

Introduction

If there is one thing I can always count on, it is the fact that if I put five or more Black women in a room—any room, any group of Black women—things are about to get real! With very little provocation or directing, we're likely going to get to the heart of things—and fast. We won't shy away from talking about relationships, parenting, racism, work, or any other topic. Deep belly laughs will be heard and knowing glances exchanged; perhaps some tears will be shed and secrets confided/imparted as well. In the sisterhood that Black women share, there is often a safety and an inherent feeling of support and acceptance that is affirming and, I believe, lifesaving.

Don't get me wrong! I know we don't live in a utopia, nor are Black women monolithic. Not all Black women want to come together and sing "Kumbaya" with one another. But without a doubt there is a cadence and rhythm to our gatherings. More often than not when we convene, there is a natural sisterhood that breeds openness, protectiveness, and a tenderness with one another: a powerful something that is hard to find in other places. Just go to Essence Fest or a Beyoncé concert, any grand gathering of Black women, and you're sure to feel it. It's an energy that cannot be duplicated. I'm also clear that this magical *thing* that Black women experience with one another is something uniquely our own. Maybe some of it has to do with our shared understanding of the challenges and traumas that exist at the intersection of race and gender. Maybe it's something that we've cultivated to create community for ourselves in the face of attempts to strip away our humanity. As interdisciplinary scholar Evelynn Hammonds says in Patricia Hill Collins's groundbreaking book *Black Feminist Thought,* "I think most of the time you have to be there to experience it. When I am with other Black women I always laugh. I think our humor comes from a shared recognition of who we all are in the world."[1] Whatever it is, to me, a gathering of Black women is sacred, it is magical, it is healing—and it has become my life's work.

I am a licensed psychologist based in Atlanta, Georgia; since 2009 I have worked with women individually as well as in group therapy settings. In 2014, I founded Therapy for Black Girls (TBG), an organization dedicated to making mental health more relevant and accessible for Black women through our podcast, therapist directory, community platform, and blog. The idea for TBG came to me after watching the BLACK GIRLS ROCK! Awards on BET. I remember being totally captivated by the program that night. From thousands of miles away, the energy of the remarkable women in that room was palpable, infectious even. Sitting on a couch in my living room, I saw women standing up—literally—to celebrate one another's achievements, shining a light on important issues and just gathering together to share their gifts as Black women. Women who excelled in areas like education, entertainment, and philanthropy were all getting and giving one another their proverbial "roses." It was truly a sight to behold. It felt warm and familiar as spaces with Black women often do. As I watched, I thought to myself, "Wouldn't it be cool to try and create something with this same kind of energy for Black women related to mental health?" The name Therapy for Black Girls came to me quite naturally, and that night I jumped on GoDaddy to purchase the domain.

When I started TBG, it was a blog where I would share posts to help make mental health topics more relevant and accessible for Black women. Because I felt that there were not enough mental health resources in the wellness industry that spoke to Black women specifically, a few of the first posts I shared were basic questions to ask a potential therapist and how to rely on your support system. I knew that there would be an audience, but to be completely honest, I was not prepared for the outpouring of sisters who were drawn to the blog and to the larger TBG community. Today, TBG has grown to include a weekly podcast that has amassed more than thirty-four million downloads, a directory of more than six thousand therapists across the United States and in Canada who love doing meaningful clinical work with Black women and girls, and—perhaps most important—a vibrant and engaged community of more than seven hundred thousand sisters around the world who have a similar goal: to work toward prioritizing their mental health and becoming the best possible versions of themselves. Of course, I didn't know it at the time, but the training and experience I've had in areas like consultation, outreach, and group therapy prepared me well for the work I've done to serve this rapt audience of Black women.

I was first introduced to the practice of facilitating therapy groups as an intern in the counseling center at Virginia Commonwealth University (VCU) in 2005. As I learned the art and nuance of leading group sessions, collectively talking through issues ranging from relationship problems to career quandaries, I fell in love with the modality and the power and possibilities of group work. In fact, I was so drawn to this form of therapy as a pathway to healing that I can draw a direct line from the work I do now to those early experiences. When I think about the current work of TBG, I conceptually view it as one long-standing, gigantic "group." The community is made up of many different types of sisters, but at the heart of it, just like the people drawn to group therapy sessions, we *all* want to be well. And as a psychologist, I am keenly aware that for Black women, wellness—and healing—often happens with and because of one another.

My approach to group therapy is also what contributes to how I facilitate the Sister Circle community I formed as a part of TBG. Every week, sisters from around the world gather on Zoom for what I call "Three for Thursday" to share their hearts and listen as we explore the topic of the week. It's also how I believe the dynamics of our personal sisterfriendships play out. We heal in community. We always have. Every Thursday afternoon when I log off that Zoom at one o'clock I am reminded of the importance of this work.

This book will ultimately explore the healing power of sisterhood and what it looks like throughout our lives and during our interactions with other sisters. I want to help you to strengthen, heal, and celebrate not just your individual friendships and your sister circle but also who we are as a collective of Black girls. As writer and playwright Ntozake Shange once said: "When I die, I will not be guilty of having left a generation of girls behind thinking that anyone can tend to their emotional health other than themselves."[2] I'm very proud of how the collective we've built acts as a harbor and a lighthouse for each of us and the sisters who follow. Every Thursday, Andrea from Massachusetts, Mary from Seattle, Paula and Dede from New York, Mona and Nia from Atlanta, and Tanya and Carla from DC come together with Jasmine in North Carolina, Melissa in Chicago, Anya in Ohio, and several other sisters from around the world. None of these sisters knew one another four years ago, but without fail, they show up weekly to hold space, offer resources, crack jokes, and worship the sacredness of sisterhood. What happens when we gather is powerful, but what fills me even more are the reverberations I trust this communion makes when they leave the space.

One of the biggest complaints I've encountered in this work is how challenging it is for many Black women to find sisterfriendships and maintain loyalty within them. Through this group, these sisters definitely learn how to be more assertive in their relationships, how to set firmer boundaries with loved ones, and even how to navigate breaking up with a therapist. Also, the evidence of care and community they demonstrate toward one another inevitably spills over into their other relationships. That is the power of the Three for Thursday space, and that is the power I hope this book helps you to create in your spaces as well. I want this book to be an extension of what I've seen happen in the group so that you walk away with a deeper understanding of the transformation that can happen in community and the tools necessary to make it happen. It is my ode to sisterhood, yes, but it is also my offering to help you heal through the connections you hold in your friendships. That is my vision for us.

I define healing as the process of revising and rewriting the difficult things that have happened to us so that they become a *part* of our story, but not the entirety of our story. Healing, especially as it relates to the experience of Black women, is operating from a place of joy rather than from the pain we may have experienced. Our sisters often give us the courage to start this process. We use sisterhood to become the best possible versions of ourselves. In this book, I want to provide you, my sister, with real-life, real-talk guidance on how to create and navigate healthy sister-friendships personally, as well as carry that direction into the world as you engage with the global sisterhood of Black women whom you may not know personally. I do not approach my therapy practice as though I have all the answers and I do not intend to frame this book that way either. At the end of the day, I'm going to share my knowledge, research, personal experiences, and observations with you in what I hope will ultimately become a dialogue between us about how sisterhood heals and how we can have a radical transformation in our friendships. This book will celebrate all the things we do well—that magical part of Black sisterhood that goes unspoken—while also challenging us with opportunities to do better. Sisterhood is such a vibrant life force for Black women. It is sacred, and as such it is important for us to pay attention to the things that make it difficult and do a better job of navigating those challenges so that it can continue to be what we need to get through the world together.

HEALING IN COMMUNITY

About sisterhood, actress and arts administrator Phylicia Rashad once said, "There is something that reverberates from us onto our communities when we return from being in community with one another."[3] Many of us have felt that, right? Our energy changes after doing the annual girls' trip with our sisters. We feel rested. Full. Whole. Our sleep feels richer after a night out with our girls. We feel empowered. Ready to take on our worlds. This isn't by accident. There's absolutely a healing aspect to the group dynamic found in our sisterhoods.

Groups are effective in large part because they lessen our feelings of isolation, provide us with multiple areas of support, and allow us to learn intimate information about ourselves that is impossible to know outside of that relationship. These are also hallmarks of sisterhood. In the richest, most fulfilling friendships we have with our sisters, there is this strong sense that we are not alone. We feel covered and protected. Even when the world is chaotic or there's been personal devastation, it's both helpful and healing to know that there are people we can go to for support and truth-telling.

As I've thought more intensely about our relationships with one another in preparing to write this book, what has become clear to me is that there are several concepts I apply as a psychologist that explain why sisterhood works the way it does and can help us flourish even more in our relationships with one another.

GROUP THERAPY AS AN APPROACH

In pop culture, we mostly see individual therapy sessions portrayed. There is one client speaking with the therapist or sometimes even a couple working with a singular counselor. What I wish we'd see more often are group therapy sessions. In my experience, group therapy is an ideal modality for many of the concerns people bring to therapy. In fact, group therapy tends to spark breakthroughs and healing that cannot happen, or at least not happen as quickly, in individual sessions. The multiple perspectives and outpouring of support would be hard to replicate. It is in a group setting that people realize something incredibly powerful—that the thing that has always felt so shameful to them is not something they struggle with alone; there are others who are feeling the same way.

Existential psychiatrist Dr. Irvin Yalom identified eleven curative factors that lead to these kinds of connections and breakthroughs in group—things that make groups work. I'll share more about them later, and if you are completely new to the modalities of therapy, don't worry. I promise not to bore you with a bunch of academic language. Instead, my goal is to highlight ways you may *already* be participating in therapeutic healing in your life and make the larger concepts feel more accessible. The last thing I want to do is overload you with theories, but it is important for you to know that the observations and guidance I'm offering here are deeply rooted not just in the foundations of psychology but also in my more than twenty years of work as a psychologist.

The bottom line? Group work can be incredibly powerful. I'll show you how your current sister circles can help serve as a place of healing for you and others through our time together. For anyone who's struggled with difficulties in relationships, the experiences you have in a group can give you the opportunity to get real-world feedback about who you are, how you show up in relationships, and the ways you can work to change past patterns. It's not always easy to be vulnerable, but by simply showing up and exposing yourself to the issues that come up for you and for the others in your circle, you may find that it can be a powerful mechanism for healing relationship wounds you've carried around for years. Group work, the ability to heal in community, teaches you a lot about yourself, your patterns, and your areas for growth. You may even find yourself taking on a familiar role in the group—one that reflects how you show up every day. (We'll also talk about this later, but the four biggies are the Leader, the Wallflower, the Firecracker, and the Peacemaker.)

As I've said, many Black women's relationships mimic some of what I've observed in group therapy sessions. Within these friend groups, each individual plays a role, and the most powerful and long-lasting sisterfriendships are the ones that allow us to feel safe in sharing our hearts and stories. In many ways, we've been doing this all along. Over the last two decades, I've worked with hundreds of clients, and I've seen them overcome the biggest hurdles, including separations in their relationships, conflicts in their friendships, personal and professional challenges, and more. We'll move through many of these in our time together.

While doing some research, I came across writer and activist Audre Lorde's essay "Eye to Eye: Black Women, Hatred, and Anger" in her 1984 book *Sister Outsider*. In it she perfectly encapsulates what sisterhood is, or could be:

> We have to consciously study how to be tender with each other until it becomes a habit because what was native has been stolen from us, the love of Black women for each other. But we can practice being gentle with ourselves by being gentle with each other. We can practice being gentle with each other by being gentle with that piece of ourselves that is hardest to hold.

Lorde so eloquently put into words the very heartbeat of this book—the stories I intend to share, the voices and experiences of the amazing women in the TBG community and beyond that, along with my own journey in sisterhood, will serve as the narrative backbone to the book. I will shine a bright light on that "thing" we know happens between us and the ways we so effortlessly, yet intentionally, show up for one another in small and large ways. The glances we share as we pass one another in public. The compliments understood only by us ("Okay, eyebrows!" or "You better wear that red lip!"). The joy and pride we feel when one of us wins. The shared history that makes it feel as though we are in constant conversation with one another without ever having to say a word.

Writing this book felt both timely and necessary. Now more

than ever, Black women seem to be longing for safe spaces to be ourselves. There's a kind of liberation we can access when we feel like there is a place we can go where we can show up authentically. But even then, there aren't many resources that can help us navigate those safe spaces, our sisterfriendships, in healthy ways. That's what I hope to do here. There are tons of books, articles, quizzes, and experts that will tell you everything you could possibly want to know about finding your life partner—what to wear on a first date, how to keep things spicy in the bedroom, etc. But there are far fewer resources about what finding and building intimacy means within the confines of friendship. My sisterfriend Nafeesa and I had many conversations while in grad school at the University of Georgia about how it was fun to date and think about married life but that sweetness was really found in our relationship with each other. The conversations we were able to have, the support, the laughter, and the ease all felt like what life partnership should really be. I've been so excited to see more sisters thinking about their relationships with their girls in this way. For all the wonderful things that can come with romantic love, our relationships with our girls are often where we really come alive. In many ways, our girls are where we can exist outside of any life role we're expected to take on. Yes, I am someone's wife. I am someone's mother. I am someone's therapist. But when I'm with my girls, I'm just with my girls as they are with me.

What is it about our friendships that allows us to exist in this way? Well, much of it is likely related to the fact that not much attention or pressure is placed on what friendships look like. From a very early age, we get messages about who we have to be as a partner, a professional, a parent, but in many ways the fact that friendships have not been seen as the center of life has allowed this space to become an untouched opportunity for us to authentically be ourselves.

While it is true that informal gatherings of women cannot necessarily replace a formal therapeutic group treatment, time after time I've found that simply being with one another *does* play a major role in our wellness. In that way, healing in these contexts is possible. Although we may know that something hurts and needs our attention, we can become intimidated by it and will often ignore it rather than confront the pain. For Black women, facing down the problem often begins in conversation with a sisterfriend. Having a sister there to sit with you and bear witness to your pain without judgment can be the space you need to face some hard and unpleasant truths.

Healing can come in surprising ways—it doesn't always have to look like heartfelt, teary-eyed, deeper than deep conversations (although it's okay if it does). What about the year you and your girls headed out of town for a long weekend and had the time of your lives? You remember how refreshed and reenergized you felt when you got back home (I mean, once you finally slept)? Y'all still talk about it to this day, don't you? That wasn't just a turn up or a "really good time"—that was healing! You remember that extended phone conversation you had with your good girlfriend whom you hadn't talked to in months that left you feeling so full of love and possibility? That was healing too! You remember how it felt to finally share that secret you thought no one would ever understand, but your girl did? Or how honored you felt when your sisterfriend became vulnerable with you for the first time, and you could just feel your relationship moving to that next level. *That was also healing!* Throughout the course of our lives, this pattern of being there for one another repeats itself over and over again—as we heal our sisters, they heal us.

THE HISTORY OF *OUR* SISTERHOOD

This pattern didn't come out of nowhere. When I began my research, I wanted to start in what seemed like the most obvious place: Africa. West Africa, specifically. I was curious as to whether the sisterhood dynamic I observed in my own lived experience and in my work as a therapist (primarily with Black women from America and the Caribbean islands) was a carryover from something our ancestors had cultivated on the continent before enslavement and colonization. Because epigenetics teaches us that our behaviors and environmental experiences can affect the way our genes work and that some of what Black people accept as part of our cultural makeup (both trauma and joy) is actually the result of transgenerational experiences that are passed down in our DNA, I assumed that the way Black women interact with one another, that *thing*, was some deeply rooted historical articulation that was imparted. If it is true that we can pass trauma and dysfunction from generation to generation, can it not also be the case that we pass joy, resilience, and connection through this same mechanism? I thought this might explain why Black women are often communal, and how that shapes the way we show up in the world today.

Well, yes and no. I was surprised to learn that the Black sisterhood dynamic in West Africa did not exactly function the way I was thinking. According to scholar Katrina Bell McDonald, author of *Embracing Sisterhood*, the idea that sisterhood existed in the ways it does today among Black women in pre-colonial Africa may not be completely accurate. McDonald notes that pre-colonial African societies operated within a dual-sex cultural system, meaning that there was power shared between men and women, and roles within the culture were assumed based on gender. Women's roles during this time focused primarily on mothering children and being mothers of the culture. In this vein, women were bound to one another in pushing forth these values, which to my mind feels like the basis of how Black culture is shared and passed on today, through the stories of Black women. McDonald goes on to say that the values of "(1) the primacy of kinship and communalism, (2) reverence for ancestors and elders, (3) respect for and practice of spirituality, the centrality of motherhood, and shared power between men and women and of gendered institutional practice where it is beneficial to the self-determination and agency of family and community"[4] are what serve as the foundation for sisterhood as we know it today. These values and the ways that pre-colonial Black women operated within this system have provided us with a framework for what is possible as we strive to forge a path forward in a post-colonial, post-slavery world.

McDonald's words feel so comforting and affirming, and they remind me of a phrase I've heard my mom repeat: "Ain't nothing new under the sun." There is no need for us to attempt to re-create the wheel. The model quite literally already exists. That said, it's important to note that while some of what we understand about Black sisterhood was inherited from pre-colonial times, most was forged during enslavement and out of need.

The value systems of communal care and shared maintenance evolved into a distinct mode of survival and thriving for Black people during enslavement and colonization. Think about the way we name one another. Within many Black communities, our friends become our cousins and our mothers' friends become our aunties. These relationships mimic the family unit in a kind of fictive kinship, and there seems to be an ancestral imprint on our souls and bodies that urges us to connect in this way. This is what was passed down. The creation of Black sisterhood as we know it is the result of our foremothers taking those ancestral values of communal engagement and, in the face of horrific trauma, re-imagining them. Allowing those values to transform into an undefinable yet deeply felt connection between us as sisters. What an amazing demonstration of resilience and interpersonal innovation! In perhaps one of the very first instances of what we now call Black girl magic, our foremothers practiced their alchemy, taking the ideals of our ancestry and turning them into a kind of relationship that could sustain and heal us.

I believe that throughout history what we see are repeated iterations of Black women forming community with one another in the interest of the values that have been discussed. In "The Impact of Same-Sex Friendships on the Well-Being of Women," an article in *Women & Therapy,* researchers note how Black women during the nineteenth century—likely post-emancipation—continued the traditions of previous generations by having mothers and aunties sharing space together after the birth of a new baby, in order to pass down "much needed motherly wisdom while also giving mom a chance to rest and breathe."[5] Communal care for the win again!

During Reconstruction in the late nineteenth century and into the first half of the twentieth century, many Black women demonstrated sisterhood through the formation of sororities. The first were born between 1908 and 1922 within what is now called the Divine Nine, or the Black Greek Letter Organizations (BGLOs). In her book *In Search of Sisterhood,* writer and professor Paula J. Giddings affirms what I'd learned about what drove Black women to reimagine how we expressed those ancient values in the context of sisterhood. During this time when young Black people were among the first in their families to attend colleges and universities, participation in organizations like a sorority were a lifeline. Against the backdrop of racism and sexism, sororities provided members with a way to build relationships and communities. The emphasis on "scholarship and achievement" countered what was experienced outside campus.

The presence of Black sororities as a way to participate in sisterhood and community, ofttimes in a world that doesn't want that for us, resonates with me personally, as one of my pathways to sisterhood was a sorority. But there are many other groups in our communities, whether formally organized like the Black church or informal like the weekly "meetup" at the hair salon, where Black women have found nurturing support systems to serve one another. And we have always had to do this, right? What other options have we had? Especially from post-Reconstruction through the Harlem Renaissance to the civil rights and Black Arts movements to the digital age of the twenty-first century, Black women are often left to gather and forge bonds with one another as we navigate increased exposure in white spaces—whether traditionally as caregivers and cleaners in white homes, or later as the first Black student in an all-white school or the first Black woman anything anywhere.

Our sisterhood has historically always been a multigenerational, intergenerational, transgenerational experience. And in the mid-twentieth century, sisterhood, even across diasporic lines, continued to be the glue for many Black women artists and activists. Marian Anderson's camaraderie and correspondence with

Black classical composer Florence Price is thought to be the impetus for the seminal presentation of "My Soul's Been Anchored in the Lord" at Anderson's historic 1939 concert on the steps of the Lincoln Memorial. Likewise, South African singer Miriam Makeba had an amazing friendship with African American singer, pianist, and activist Nina Simone. Makeba's politics were very much in relationship with how she engaged in sisterhood, according to "Black Sisterhood in Music," an article in the online magazine *AMAKA Studio*.[6] She was a woman who used her music to fight against apartheid in South Africa in many of the same ways Nina Simone used her music to fight against Jim Crow segregation in America. They even collaborated on a song about Black womanhood, "Thulasizwe / I Shall Be Released," and remained close friends throughout their lives.

The necessity for Black women to have the opportunities and spaces to nurture sisterhood has expanded greatly over the last fifty years. We only have to look as far as the Black Is Beautiful movements of the seventies and the natural hair movement revival of the late nineties to realize that we've always mobilized ourselves around our shared need for safe spaces that reflect our unique way of being. I'm reminded of a couple of #TBT photos that have made the internet rounds recently. One of my favorites is a black-and-white picture of several now-revered Black women writers, who called themselves The Sisterhood, posing together, some with wide smiles and wider Afros and all with a knowing in their eyes. The image features Toni Morrison, Alice Walker, Ntozake Shange, June Jordan, Lori Sharpe, and Audrey Edwards at a meeting for Black women writers in 1971. Clearly, they are all in the early stages of their careers, and yet there's something about the way they are standing with one another that denotes a closeness or, at the very least, an understanding.

Seventeen years later, another photo delivers those same feelings of sisterhood and camaraderie. In this 1988 image, Gwendolyn Brooks, Toni Cade Bambara, Sonia Sanchez, Nikki Giovanni, and Mari Evans are posing in a larger group of Black women writers. Seeing these women whose books I've read and whose stories I've savored standing together, supporting one another, feels like an indication that even within tight-knit Black literary circles, there was a desire to connect and hold space for their sisters. The love was palpable, and recognizable.

Whether it's an image of Toni Morrison and Angela Davis walking down the street in New York City or a candid snapshot of elders Toni Morrison and Maya Angelou at an awards ceremony caught in the middle of what must have been many kikis over their forty-year friendship—these moments all lead me to the same conclusion: That *thing* Black women feel when we gather is a kind of glue, a stabilizing force we actively created out of the pain and trauma of our lived experiences in order to hold us up and together. It's in the way we laugh and cry and fuss and holler about an episode of *Insecure* (#TeamIssa or #TeamMolly) or how we share our eggs and sugar with the mama next door because sometimes life shows up rocky and maybe we've all been there. No matter where we find ourselves individually in life, we generally always find a way to love on and support another sister in some way.

Historically, and until the present day, sisterhood is a modern Black woman's birthright. Sure, we all have a choice as to whether we will accept it. I will explore in later chapters why some of us might not choose sisterhood in the ways many of us have experienced it. But one thing remains true: It is ours. We do not have to do anything but exist to be part of this powerful network of support.

WHY THIS BOOK? WHY NOW?

In the chapters that follow, I will share stories that are actually composite narratives derived from focus group conversations and interviews conducted for the book. In part 1, I will unpack the importance of connecting with others and how our relationships with other Black women are shaped by our early experiences. We'll explore how our sisterfriendships have been essential for our survival. I'll also examine what psychology, and group therapy in particular, can teach us about having strong relationships with one another. In part 2, we'll examine what it means to hold space for our sisters and the role that vulnerability plays in our ability to do just that. Part 3 will dive deeper into the conflicts and barriers that get in the way of our sisterhoods being successful. We will also tend to what it means when our sisterfriendships end and how we grieve them. As we close, in part 4, I will share strategies for finding new sisters to connect with and what it takes to navigate sisterhood online. This section will also outline what it means to be more intentional with the sisters in your life and in your community, to truly practice sisterhood. I firmly believe that what you learn in this book will help you heal your relationships, which will ultimately mean you'll be healing yourself. You will walk away from this book with a greater sense of how you show up in your friendships, what you want from those relationships, and how to navigate both the highs and the lows of sisterhood.

In a world where Black women so often feel invisible, I hope you will see yourself in these pages. I hope you smile, laugh, and nod your head in agreement (but it's okay to shake your head in disagreement too!). I hope this book connects you to that special *thing* that exists between us. As bell hooks writes, "Rarely, if ever, are any of us healed in isolation. Healing is an act of communion."[7] That thing between us is our path to healing. I'm so honored that you have chosen this book at this time, and that you will take this journey with me. I got you. And we got us.

Sisterhood Heals

PART I

The Foundations of Connection

Sisterhood is a funny thing.
It's easy to recognize, but hard to define.

–*Pearl Cleage*

CHAPTER 1

What Shapes Our Connections

We are each other's harvest; / we are each other's business;
/ we are each other's magnitude and bond.

—Gwendolyn Brooks

My grandparents' home sits at what I would describe as the apex of the little town of Napoleonville, Louisiana. It is directly across the street from a Baptist church, up the street from the elementary school, around the corner from the house where you could buy the best homemade pies, and on the route to the only grocery store there was in town until it closed after Hurricane Katrina. In short, it is a great place to have a front row seat to all the action, and the best seats were always on the front porch, where the women in my family "held court."

Like the ear-hustling kindergartner I was, the porch was also where I wanted to be. It's where the women in my family would gather, whether they were eating frozen cups or doing hair. It's where my Tee Jane would talk about whose kids were acting up at school and my Tee Cynt would talk about the latest employment drama at Bill's Dollar Store. It's where my Tee Ivy would get caught up on all the latest town gossip since she now lived in Texas and was usually only home for the summer and Christmas. Tee Lisa would take a sip of Dr Pepper—mostly for dramatic effect—before filling us, I mean them, in on what she'd heard while getting her hair done.

"Y'all heard Reverend Arnold's sons was down there fighting at Blue Monday?" Tee Lisa would ask.

"Fighting! What were they fighting for?" Tee Cynt wondered aloud.

"Apparently that youngest one, Darryl, found Cedric Wilson's car in the driveway when he came back from offshore, and you know that didn't go over too well."

"Oh no! Didn't his wife just have that baby a few months ago?"

Hiding behind the door or hovering unseen somewhere nearby, with the tiny hairs on my five-year-old arms standing at attention, I'd peep around the corner to listen as she expertly weaved the harrowing tale of what happened when Darryl came back home to find Cedric alone with his wife. "Girl, yeah. They said he took off on foot running straight down Highway 308. He lucky he didn't get hit."

"I know them neighbors was outside cutting up."

"You know they were!"

The cackles and laughter as she relayed Cedric's attempts to run out of the house unscathed did something to my little body that I wouldn't be able to define for decades. Though I didn't always understand what they were talking about or what was going on when my aunts and grandmother would have these porch talks, I knew it was something special. There were always laughs, always somebody talking loudly, or whispering if the occasion called for it. All I knew was that this dynamic, this back-and-forth way of being, of engaging, was everything. It was where I first learned the healing power of sisterhood. It's also the first place I learned how to navigate conflict. It was the sharing between these women in my life that provided a foundation for what I understood sisterhood to be.

Over the course of our lives, we build the foundations of our connections on inherited ideas about what it means to be in relationship with one another, how to deal with differences between ourselves and others, and who is deemed worthy of such connection. Those earliest ideas about connection, community, and sisterhood as well as *how* we attach ourselves to one another are often formed in our youth. They evolve from our very first relationships, with our parents or caregivers, siblings, and family members. In order to truly unpack, heal, and grow our friendships and ourselves we must start at our origin stories.

Some of the most formidable conversations I have with my clients stem from the information they share about their early relationships. I often spend time asking them questions and listening to their responses: Who was your biggest supporter growing up? How would you describe your relationship with your parents? How would you describe your relationships with your siblings? What did your friendships look like as a child? What I'm listening for are patterns in relationship dynamics from childhood that might be impacting current relationships. For example, a response like "No one really supported me growing up" or "I made friends pretty easily but none of the friendships seemed to last" would likely prompt a conversation about what support looks like today and whether longevity in friendships continues to be difficult. By no means does our childhood write our future in stone, but it can provide some helpful clues.

Because of the salience of women's friendships in our lives, it is important for me to assess this as a part of my work. Our friendships, our sister circles, have been proven to extend the years of our lives. This isn't hyperbole, Sis. It's true! In fact, Dr. Robin Dunbar, an anthropologist and evolutionary psychologist, states that "friendship is the single most important factor influencing our health, well-being, and happiness."[1] There's no way around it—we need one another. We need our sisters. Psychologist Julianne Holt-Lunstad and her colleagues found that being isolated was as bad for our health as smoking fifteen cigarettes per day.[2] And Harvard Medical School agrees. Its 2010 study showed that "a relative lack of social ties is associated with depression and later-life cognitive decline, as well as with increased mortality."[3]

In addition to all the studies about how affirming friendships and connections are to improved physical health and longer life expectancy, it's also true that relationships with our sisters can contribute to greater self-esteem and stronger mental health. Healthy friendships make us feel less lonely, and that has a huge overall impact. Much has also been written and shared about the staggering effect that loneliness can have on our lives. In 2019, the Cigna U.S. Loneliness Index reported that 61 percent of Americans shared feeling lonely. That same year, a study of two thousand Americans, commissioned by Evite, found that the average American hadn't made a new friend in the past five years. Loneliness has been linked to elevated risk of heart disease, higher blood pressure, and increased rates of depression and anxiety.[4]

Forming strong connections with others—physical, mental, and emotional bonds that can withstand time and change—is not only valuable in many areas of our lives but also integral to our development as humans and connected to our very survival. For Black women, this is especially true. It is why I believe that the best way for Black women to thrive is through our healthy relationships with other Black women. As Nikki Giovanni once said, "Black women are . . . the only group that derives its identity from itself. I think it's been rather unconscious but we measure ourselves by ourselves, and I think that's a practice we can ill afford to lose."[5] Yes ma'am, Ms. Giovanni. I couldn't agree more. I measured so much of myself by those women I loved on the porch. But I'm also clear that keeping close ties and maintaining flourishing relationships as an adult is not always so easy. The hurdles tend to have deeper roots.

MESSAGES FROM MAMA

"What did Sheena say to you yesterday?" my mama would say. Or, her favorite question was "Do you think she's jealous of you?" From the time I started high school until now, my mother has always been intrusive in my relationships with other girls and women. She wants to know everything— I mean, every single detail. She's always cautioning me to be wary of my friends because she believes that women, in general, are not trustworthy. In her words, "They will turn on you in a minute." I don't necessarily believe that, but I have to admit that her questions often left me confused. I gravitated to having more friendships with guys because it just didn't create the kind of friction with Mom as the relationships with girlfriends did.

—Tamara, 35

Do you recognize any of your own story in Tamara's? I certainly do. The sentiments she shared are ones I've heard before, both in my own family and from women in the TBG community.

We're often taught which girls are worthy of friendship and what women might stain our own image; these are all preconceived notions based not on fact but, dare I say, more on fear. As for me, and maybe you too, I was taught to steer clear of the "fast girl" growing up. What this warning actually did was put a certain type of woman on a pedestal of acceptance, and, over time, these same inherited beliefs about worth kept us from making connections with sisters who could have helped us to grow and served as lifelines. Receiving these warning messages seems to be a very distinct experience for Black women, as opposed to other groups. Professors of social work Geoffrey L. Greif and Tanya L. Sharpe write about their 2010 study of these relationships in "The Friendships of Women: Are There Differences Between African Americans and Whites?": "Another difference among the two groups is that the African American women were much more likely to say they heard cautionary tales about female friends from their mothers. Roughly one-third received advice about not lending money to friends, not letting too many women into the home, and not keeping friends too close (a reference to their trustworthiness) . . . None of the White women reported hearing cautionary tales from their mothers." Thus, we are left believing strongly that [Black] women are influenced by the direct and subliminal messages received from their mothers' friendships.[6] Where's the lie? Are you able to identify any messages about other women that you carry with you from childhood or that you've had to release as you have begun to heal? I know I can.

If you were a Black girl or woman who listened to hip-hop in the late nineties and early aughts, you likely remember precisely where you were the first few times you heard the strums of that plucky baseline. Its rhythm and syncopation might have even sounded like your own heartbeat. Those smooth violin strings in the background and then the whispered "Hah, hah" created an anticipation and excitement that got you poised like a track star ready to leap off the starting block. But it's only when Juvenile said "Cash Money Records takin' over for the '99 and the 2000" that you actually took off. Maybe you ran to the dance floor. Maybe you let your body do what it wanted to do right there in your seat. No matter what, you moved and danced like Y2K was real and dropping it like it was hot was the only way you'd survive. (Maybe for you it's "Flash Light" by Parliament or even Megan Thee Stallion's "Body.")

Now, some of us took Juvenile's petition for us to "back that thang up" way more seriously than others. I know my friend Nicole did. When the song came on while we were in college, she'd lose her whole, entire mind. I loved watching her kill it on the dance floor at whatever party we were at, but that hadn't always been the case. Before coming to college, I wasn't much of a fan of Nicole's, mostly for that exact reason. We'd first met a few years earlier after attending several camps together in my senior year of high school. She was friendly enough, but my Spidey-senses started to tingle when I would see the way she danced with the boys at our social events. Let's just say I'm sure Tamara's mama would have a mouthful to say about her. At the Student Council Camp in Natchitoches, I'll never forget watching her do these choreographed dances that felt way too "grown" for us high schoolers. There I was doing my cute little two-step in our uniform of matching white T-shirt and jean shorts, and Sis would be swinging her hair back and dropping her whole booty to the floor, making all the boys lose it of course. Back then, though, I didn't watch in admiration or celebration as I would when we were in college. I spent most of my time judging her. Hard. In my mind, she was what my mother called a "fast girl" and I avoided her like my life depended on it.

I don't remember exactly how old I was when my mama first warned me about being "fast." I think it was probably in middle school before a school dance. At the time, I didn't really know what it meant but could surmise that it was something related to being too flirty with boys. The fear of being fast not only governed my behavior but also impacted my ideas about other girls and who they were. Nicole would ultimately become one of my closest friends during my first year at Xavier University. I would later find out that she had been a dancer for most of her life and that if what she did looked choreographed, it probably was. When we became friends, I eventually told her how I felt about her that summer and she was surprised because, in her mind, she was just dancing. It's something she still teases me about until this day.

Now what would have happened if I hadn't let go of my pre-conceived notions of who Nicole was? I'll tell you. I would have missed out on someone who I can count on no matter what. Someone I have called when the "ish" hit the fan and, without hesitation, she rode out to pick me up, no questions asked. She is one of the only people I trust with my children. She takes care of them if my husband and I are away, and she's listed as an emergency contact at their school. Our kids play soccer together and go to baseball games together. Ideally, they will grow up and consider one another important parts of their support system.

I share this story because in many ways it illustrates how the early messages we get about other sisters impact us years later. Just like Tamara, many of us have experiences with our moms, aunties, grandmothers, or other women in our lives who have warned us to be wary of other women, that they are not to be trusted, that they are not safe, that they do not mean us well. If we've grown up with these ideas, then it stands to reason that as adults we may have trouble building sustaining connections with other Black women. I wonder if you might need to reconsider a sister in your life because you've held on to a story about her that isn't true. Are there reactions you have to other Black women that you might now reassess because they don't tell the whole story?

Hearing sisters say they get along better with men or describe themselves as a "guys' girl" often gives me pause. When this is expressed, my immediate question is always "What happened?" as their description of themselves usually comes from having experienced painful and traumatic relationships with other sisters. These feelings frequently develop from experiences like being teased or bullied, being betrayed by a sister, or not observing affirming and reciprocal relationships between other Black women and girls. This said, I submit that one of the true gifts of sisterhood is the ability to revise this script with and for one another. We have the ability to provide one another with a corrective emotional experience. In therapy, we do this by creating a safe space for clients to share themselves and receive responses different from the ones they are used to getting.

Let's look at an example: Jessica is a twenty-three-year-old Black woman client who struggles with not feeling good enough because of messages she received as a child from her parents and other adults in her life. She was often yelled at when she made mistakes and otherwise criticized for her grades and behavior. In her work with me, her tenderness around not feeling good enough was activated when she forgot to show up for a session once because she wasn't feeling well. It was unlike her not to call if she needed to cancel an appointment, so when I asked her about it the following week she apologized profusely and made remarks about being a "bad client" and wasting my time. I responded by saying that it was not a problem that she missed the appointment and that I was glad she stayed home to prioritize her health. She began to cry. When asked what was stirring for her she shared that typically her mistakes are met with criticism and that she expected the same from me. The fact that I did not react the way others in her life did gave her an opportunity to see that mistakes could be handled in other ways and that though she had made a mistake, she was not the mistake.

THE WAY WE ATTACH

A significant amount of research has been done to further explore the roots of our connections and offer ways to turn them around so that we may have fulfillment in our present-day relationships. Psychologists John Bowlby and Mary Ainsworth developed an evolutionary thesis known as attachment theory that greatly informs what we know about our connections with others. I think it's so important to begin here because by investigating how we learned to connect with people early on, we can then evaluate areas in our lives where we thrive as well as areas that need improvement. We can pinpoint why we respond to our friends in a particular way and begin to do the work to heal, if that's what's needed. Ultimately, this will make all our relationships—especially the ones with our sisters—better.

Attachment theory proposes that when our needs are tended to and our caregivers are responsive to us as babies, we develop a sense of security that allows us to depend on those in our lives. If, however, we are not tended to and caregivers are not responsive, we may become more anxious and less secure, therefore making it difficult to reliably depend on others. The easiest example of this shows up in the responsiveness of parents to their baby's cries. Or in how quickly hunger is addressed. Children learn early on whether they can depend on their caregivers to attend to their basic physical and emotional needs. Although this development takes place very early in life, it often shapes what we feel about relationships with others throughout our lives. While the early work of Bowlby and Ainsworth measured attachment categorically (secure vs. insecure) and primarily focused on the early relationship between child and caregiver, current research has shifted to measure adult attachment styles as a function of scores in two dimensions: attachment avoidance and attachment anxiety. Higher scores in both dimensions suggest a more insecure attachment style while lower scores are indicative of a more secure attachment style.

Attachment theory is at work in our lives all the time and it often goes unnoticed. It shows up in our assumptions about a friend who might be a tad distant ("She's so standoffish"), or when we constantly wear the cape of "strong friend" in our relationships and are never fully vulnerable ("Girl, I'm fine"). It rears its head when we become angry that our sister hasn't responded to our text ("I know good and well she didn't leave me on read!"). Let's see how.

ATTACHMENT AVOIDANCE AND ATTACHMENT ANXIETY

INSECURE ATTACHMENT

High Attachment Avoidance	High Attachment Anxiety
• Minimal effort in developing and/or sustaining close relationships • Uncomfortable with intimacy • Engages in behavior to keep relationships at a distance	• Frequent worry about being abandoned by others • Exerts significant effort to maintain relationships, can sometimes come off as smothering or clingy

SECURE ATTACHMENT

Low Attachment Avoidance	Low Attachment Anxiety
• Comfortable relying on others • Seeks out the support of others during difficult times	• Confident about the health of relationships with others • Minimal worry about losing friends

Attachment avoidance reflects our comfort in relying on others. If we are lower in terms of attachment avoidance, we are more likely to be comfortable relying on others and having them rely on us. Additionally, those with lower attachment avoidance seek out the support of others during difficult times and are comfortable with more intimacy and closeness in relationships.

If we are highly avoidant, we are less likely to put effort into developing and/or sustaining close relationships because we may not feel this is possible and may not be comfortable with the level of intimacy required in a close relationship. Those who are highly avoidant may also engage in behaviors that keep others at a distance to avoid intimacy. It is not that those who are highly avoidant do not want or need connections; they are often just uncomfortable with having the need and don't always understand what it takes to keep them. In my work, high attachment avoidance often manifests as someone struggling with a traumatic experience who tries to "protect" herself by changing the subject every time it comes up at brunch with the girls from work who have been trying to get close to her ("Oh enough about me . . ."). Recent research expands on this issue as it relates to Black women by noting that "as a result of continuously conjuring resilience as a response to physical and psychological hardships, many Black women have mastered the art of portraying strength while concealing trauma—a balancing act often held in high esteem among Black women."[7] So even if we really want Sis to open up, we get why she doesn't. And some of us even applaud her for "being strong" when the truth is that she's strong *and* avoidant.

Ouch, Dr. Joy! Get off my toes.

I know, I know. Don't worry, though. I'm going to give you some tools to begin working on that.

If you recognize yourself as someone who may have a higher level of attachment avoidance (let's say you are the sister who gets uncomfortable when it looks like the friendship is getting deeper), here are a few things to consider that may help you navigate your friendships:

1. Take a long hard look at how you might be getting in your own way. In what small or large, conscious or subconscious, ways are you pushing people away, being overly critical, or demonstrating a lack of care and/or effort?

2. Let people love you. If you're honest with yourself, there are probably at least two sisters you can call right now who would be at your home in no time if you flashed the Bat-Signal! You don't have to wait until you're in a crisis to let them in; start with a small ask. Can they come over to help you finally get your office organized or to just sit with you while you fold the mountain of clothes you've been avoiding?

3. Watch your mouth and your thoughts. If you tend to frequently search for distance, you could find yourself saying things that, while true, may not be compassionate. Likewise, you may find yourself assuming the worst about a situation without checking for accuracy. Try slowing these processes down to help narrow the distancing. Check in with yourself to see if there's a kinder way to share the thing that needs to be said and check with others to see if the story you've created about an event is accurate.

A gentle note for the sister who finds herself in a relationship with a sister who is highly avoidant: Be intentional about meeting her needs without her having to ask. Demonstrations of reliability can help to foster a sense of interdependence. In this case, a little can go a long way.

Attachment anxiety, on the other hand, reflects our worry about being abandoned by others. If we are lower in terms of anxiety, we typically do not have the constant worries about being abandoned in the relationship. This is the friend who isn't concerned when another sister is introduced to the friend group. She also doesn't create narratives in her mind about losing her friendships just because someone new has entered the picture.

If scores in this area reflect higher anxiety, there may be a significant effort in maintaining a close relationship accompanied by a significant level of worry about losing the relationship. When we are highly anxious, our worries about being abandoned by those close to us can often show up in behaviors that are smothering and signify high levels of distress. When we are more anxious in this area there also tends to be a more negative self-appraisal, feeling as though we are not worthy or of value.

This attachment anxiety likely began in childhood. Maybe you had an absentee parent who never showed up to any of your most important events—band recital, prom send-off, graduation—and now whenever a friend constantly reschedules getting together you think it has more to do with you than her own situation. Instead of taking your friend at her word, you build an entire story about why she probably doesn't want to get together because of some perceived flaw that only you have about yourself: *I bet you I talked too much about my boyfriend the last time we got together and now she doesn't want to hear it.*

No, Sis. She's probably had to work late to catch up from being away on vacation for two weeks. Like. She. Said.

Having a high level of attachment anxiety can reverberate throughout our adult lives if we aren't careful and aware. But there is hope in turning things around! If you recognize yourself as someone who may have a higher level of attachment anxiety, here are a few things to consider that may be helpful in your friendships:

1. Be honest with yourself about who you are and the needs you have in friendships. There is no sense in trying to pretend you don't need what you do need or trying to minimize it. Being honest with yourself first and then with friends can increase your chances of actually getting what you need out of the friendship. Additionally, it can be important to verbalize how you're feeling to others so that they have some context for the behaviors you may engage in to receive reassurance. It's okay to say to a friend, "Hey, I know that at times I can come off as needy. I realize this can be off-putting, but I appreciate your patience as I work on this area in my life and I'm okay with you gently calling it to my attention when I may not realize it."

2. Seek out and cultivate friendships with those who help you to feel more secure. If you're already aware that you're someone who needs lots of reassurance and affirmation in a friendship, perhaps think twice about forming a deeper connection with the sister who's already showing signs of being inconsistent.

3. It may also be a good idea to learn a few self-soothing techniques that you can use when you find yourself activated and feeling worried about the friendship. One of my favorites is a grounding exercise called 5-4-3-2-1. The purpose of the exercise is to connect you with your five senses so that you are grounded in the current moment, which short-circuits your ability to worry about the past or the future. For the exercise, sit up comfortably in a chair or on the side of your bed with your feet planted on the floor. Take a few moments to notice
5 things in your environment that you can see,
4 things in your environment that you can feel,
3 things in your environment that you can hear,
2 things in your environment that you can smell, and
1 thing in your environment that you can taste.
The goal here is not to create any stories about any of the things you notice, but simply to notice them.

Secure attachment is best characterized as having a high level of comfort in relying on others and a low level of worry about being abandoned, while insecure attachment is characterized as having a low level of comfort in relying on others and a high level of worry about being abandoned. At the core of secure attachment is trust. We must be able to trust that when we need help, someone will help. We must be able to trust that when we are less than perfect, we won't be shamed. We must be able to trust that who we are, just as we are, is a lovable and valuable person. Trusting that all these things are true means that we believe that we are enough.

And that belief allows us to move through a world that is often chaotic and out of our control with a sense of inner peace.

Fortunately (or unfortunately, for some of us), the first place we learn whether who we are is enough is from our relationships. The people in our early lives whom we trust to care for us often have the power to determine whether we will believe that we are enough later on. Their actions can either ground us in a solid sense of self—enoughness, if you will—or leave us feeling uncertain and, yes, insecure about who we are and what we can offer the world. In addition to our experiences with our individual caregivers as children, if we consider the impact of marginalization and other systemic challenges on Black women and, as a result, the lack of trust that's often passed down transgenerationally, then it makes sense that some of us might lean toward an insecure attachment style. In fact, according to research conducted by Dr. LaToya Hampton, "the transmission of generational trauma continues to affect the Black community. It acts as a barrier for good mental health practices, secure attachments, overall physical health, and effective parenting styles."[8]

All hope is not lost though, Sis.

While a significant amount of how we relate to others is shaped by our early experiences with parents and caregivers, that does not mean that there can be no change in our attachment styles. Research[9] has shown that we can develop a more secure attachment style in a variety of ways, one of them being through our connections to surrogate attachment figures, which for many of us are our sister circles. Though early experiences with parents may have been unreliable and inconsistent, relationships later in life can teach us that we are worthy of care and consideration and that people can and will be there to love and support us.

When we feel safer in newer relationships and people have shown us that we can rely on them, it opens up many opportunities for trying out new behaviors. This is yet another example of the corrective emotional experience I discussed earlier. In addition to our connections with surrogate attachment figures, therapy has also been shown to be an effective means of developing a more secure attachment style.[10] Consistent meetings with a supportive professional where you are encouraged to ask for help, receive the help, and are not shamed for having needs in the first place can be a life-changing experience if we have not received this type of care before.

WHAT WE LEARN ABOUT RELATIONSHIPS THROUGHOUT LIFE

I know what I'm about to say is probably *the* biggest cliché thing heard from a therapist and something I've repeated over and over again. In fact, I'm sure it is and I know I have. But it's nonetheless true: Everything starts with our earliest experiences. How we move through the world is informed by what we were taught, how we were treated, and what resources we had access to as a child. So that's why I'm spending some time here with all of these theories around early development. If we truly want to understand why having sisterfriendships is so important and why we should be willing to work at sustaining those relationships, then we must understand our earliest encounters and how they have impacted us.

Researchers have studied our relational development for a good portion of the last century and what they've found is that at every stage of our lives we move through periods that can either strengthen our approach to friendship and relationships or, at times, harm how we engage. The theory of psychosocial development proposed by German American psychologist Erik Erikson suggests that our personalities are developed by encountering eight developmental stages throughout our lives. At each stage, we're given the opportunity to move toward that "enoughness" I mentioned earlier—a kind of self-acceptance or even actualization—or in the opposite direction toward insecurity and shame and fear-based engagements with the world. Let's take a quick look at the stages.

Stage Number	Age Range	Development Stage
1	Infant	Trust vs. Mistrust
2	Toddler	Autonomy vs. Shame
3	Preschooler	Initiative vs. Guilt
4	Ages 5–12	Industry vs. Inferiority
5	Teenager	Identity vs. Role Confusion
6	Ages 18–40	Intimacy vs. Isolation
7	Ages 40–65	Generativity vs. Stagnation
8	Senior	Ego Integrity vs. Despair

Erikson believed that as we advance through each stage, we have the opportunity to learn valuable skills that assist us in mastering future stages. For instance, if our earliest experiences teach us that we can trust the people who are charged with loving and caring for us, then this increases the likelihood that we approach our friendships with that same kind of optimism (barring any intervening trauma). Our ability to navigate through or master a stage gives insight into our relationships with others and how we interact with the world. When it comes to our sisterfriendships, stage 6, Intimacy vs. Isolation, is particularly important. During this stage, the task is to form loving and intimate relationships with others. Mastery of this stage leads to feelings of fulfillment and security. For our purposes, it means that your sister circle is tight and right. You have a core group of friends and family with whom you have good, healthy relationships. You have people who love and care about you, and you love and care about them. You're actively in a community.

Difficulties with navigating this stage may lead to experiences of isolation and feeling disconnected. It is clear that having lasting and healthy connections with others is important to our health and well-being, but it's also important to look at the areas that impact the shape these connections take. As I mentioned earlier, time and time again I've seen that connections for Black women are shaped by the messages we receive from our mothers and other women in our lives about other Black women, and by our attachment styles.

GROWING OUR CONNECTIONS

In sisterhood, we create corrective emotional experiences for one another by building and engaging in relationships that are affirming, trustworthy, and spacious. We do this by showing up when we say we will, by extending grace when mistakes happen, and by apologizing when we hurt someone. Being intentional in these ways allows trust to be built and rebuilt. By allowing ourselves to *be seen* and to truly *see* other Black women, we can soothe painful histories and provide one another with alternative endings to the stories that have typically hurt us.

Armed with the information we need to better understand how our current connections have formed, let us now turn our attention to how we can continue to grow and cultivate them. As you can probably tell from the number of times I've asked you to engage in self-assessment, I think that any good plan has to first start with an assessment. We have to get the lay of the land to know what's currently happening before we decide what to do next. The journey to solid and healthy relationships with our sisters is no different. I've created the Sisterhood Health Survey (see page 25) to help you take stock of the current state of your relationships; it will be helpful as we continue our time together. The survey is based on my belief in what I call the 4 *S*s of Sisterhood that help us thrive in our relationships. In my work with hundreds of clients and with the thousands of sisters in the TBG community, these tenets have come up over and over again when I hear Black women talk about the value of their relationships with other sisters.

THE 4 SS OF SISTERHOOD

Sisterhood allows us to be seen. Do you remember how your mama could tell something was wrong with you just from the tone of your voice? I believe our sisters possess some of this magic as well. Despite all of our attempts to hide, they create spaces to affirm and celebrate our fullness. When you find yourself questioning whether or not you are qualified for a particular position or opportunity, it's often your sister who will hype you up and tell you to be all you can be. She's the one who is going to run the receipts of your résumé to remind you of your awesomeness. So many experiences in our lives teach us to shrink ourselves, to be invisible. It is often safer that way; it feels uncomfortable to be seen. But in our sister circles we are embraced and validated as we are.

Sisterhood allows us to support and be supported. No one knows the difficulty of asking for help like another Black woman. When it's so easy to fall into an "Eff it, I'll do it myself" mentality, sisterhood allows us to practice asking for and receiving help. It allows us to pour into one another in a way only we can. I've seen many women transition from the "If I don't do it, it won't get done right" type of person to "What does this look like as a team effort?" simply by feeling safe enough to ask for help from those in her friend group.

Sisterhood allows for greater knowledge of self. Because we do not exist in this world in isolation, much of what we know about who we are comes through our connections and relationships to others. Sisterhood allows us to try out new behaviors, experiment with new identities, ask questions without judgment, and expand our ideas about what is possible. All of these things help us get clearer about who we are and what we value. Expanding our sister circle to include a diversity of ages is also crucial as it allows for deeper insight about ourselves based on what sisters older and younger than us have gone through.

Sisterhood allows us to soften. Quickly, what song do you play to hype yourself up before going into that meeting you know will be tense? Don't be scared to share! Mine is "Never Scared" by Bone Crusher. If you know, you know! So many of the spaces we inhabit require us to put on armor, and that can take its toll on us mentally, emotionally, and physically. If you watched the Supreme

Court nomination hearings for Justice Ketanji Brown Jackson, it was clear that she too had to wrestle with herself before sitting in front of a group of people who obviously were trying to "catch her slipping." The way we frequently have to steel ourselves in order to be sure-footed in the face of criticism and often flat-out disrespect is far too common. After adorning yourself in armor to face the world, what a respite it is to figuratively "take off your bra" in a safe space with your girls. With one another, there is no need for hardness.

Sisterhood Health Survey

Spend some time in your journal reflecting on your friendships, then evaluate your relationships with your sisters by examining the truth of the statements in the chart below. You can choose to conduct a separate survey for each individual friend or for your friend group as a whole. Score each statement on a scale from 1 (never true) to 5 (always true).

BEING SEEN

	1 Never True	2 Rarely True	3 Unsure	4 Sometimes True	5 Always True
I can be my authentic self around my friend(s).					
When conflicts occur, my friend(s) know how to resolve them well.					
I can share parts of myself or my story with my friend(s) that I typically would keep hidden.					
My friend(s) value my opinion.					

BEING SUPPORTED

	1 Never True	2 Rarely True	3 Unsure	4 Sometimes True	5 Always True
My friend(s) will show up for me and keep promises. I can count on my friend(s) to be reliable.					
My friend(s) will find ways to care for me in times of need/ when I need it.					
In a crisis situation, I can call on my friend(s) for help.					
I am comfortable asking my friend(s) for help.					

BEING YOURSELF

	1 Never True	2 Rarely True	3 Unsure	4 Sometimes True	5 Always True
I feel good and most like myself when I spend time with my friend(s).					
I've learned so much about myself as a result of having the friend(s) I do.					
I wish I had some of the same qualities as my friend(s).					
My friend(s) will help expand my vision for myself and what I want for my life.					

BEING SOFTER

	1 Never True	2 Rarely True	3 Unsure	4 Sometimes True	5 Always True
I can trust that my friend(s) won't make me feel ashamed if I'm vulnerable.					
I do not feel judged by my friend(s).					
My friend(s) and I share the responsibility of care for each other. It is a reciprocal relationship.					
I have amazing "play time" with my friend(s).					

CHECK YOURSELF

	1 Never True	2 Rarely True	3 Unsure	4 Sometimes True	5 Always True
My friend(s) can be vulnerable around me without being shamed.					
My friend(s) won't feel judged by me.					
My friend(s) feel seen and supported by me.					
I find ways to show up for my friend(s) in times of need.					

REFLECTING ON YOUR RESPONSES

What was it like to complete this exercise? Perhaps it became clearer to you just how solid your girls are or perhaps you learned that some areas need improvement. It's possible you learned that there's some work you need to do to show up differently in your sister circle. All information is good information because it provides us with clarity. I don't want you to feel bad about any of the areas that need work. I just want you to be open to the process of growing. As we move throughout this book, you'll learn ways to improve on the areas that may need it and ways to strengthen the areas that are already working.

If most of your responses were *Always True* or *Sometimes True*, it sounds like you have a pretty solid sister or group of sisters in your corner. You likely feel seen and supported in these relationships and are comfortable being yourself. You all have probably been through some tough times together and have seen one another through them. Questions to explore: What about this relationship do I find most fulfilling? What areas might make this relationship even stronger? The truth is, I'm writing this book for those who have sisterhood on lock too. Our friendships can never be too healthy or life-giving.

If most of your answers were *Unsure* or *Rarely True*, it sounds like there's something promising with this sister or group of sisters but perhaps you all haven't settled into a groove yet. Perhaps you find yourself initiating most of the contact or for some reason you feel hesitant to talk with her or them about certain things. Perhaps it's a newer relationship and you're still learning about each other. Questions to explore: What reservations do I have about this relationship? Do I see the potential for this relationship to become more intimate? Are there conflicts I'm ignoring and if so, why?

If most of your answers were *Never True*, it sounds like there may be some things to discuss with this sister or your friend group. It may be that you don't feel valued in the relationship. Are you helping this sister or group out of a crisis but not feeling like you can turn to her or them for help? Perhaps there's been a major disagreement or conflict and even though you've tried to talk it out, no resolution has occurred. Questions to explore: Do I like who I am and how I feel in the presence of this person or group? What changes need to be made for this relationship to feel fulfilling for me?

QUESTIONS FOR REFLECTION

1. What messages about Black women did you learn from your mother or other women in your family? How have they shaped your interactions and relationships with sisters?

2. How would you describe your attachment style, and how do you think it impacts the way you show up in your sister circle?

3. What benefits have you received from sisterhood? How do your relationships with other Black women enhance your life?

CHAPTER 2

The Whole Is Greater than the Sum of Its Parts

I think when Black women are together,
a sacred space can be conjured.

–*Ava DuVernay*

Much of the work that happens in Therapy for Black Girls is centered on the principles of group therapy for a reason. In therapeutic communities, we are able to share our stories, offer valuable resources, and serve as pillars of support for one another. Likewise, in our sisterhoods, we are mirrors for one another, reflecting back not only the parts of us we adore but also the parts of us we'd rather hide. How many of us have figured out that the thing that gets on our last nerve about our sisterfriend is probably something we also need to work on? Go on and raise your hand, Sis. I'd raise mine if I weren't typing. Of course, the goal is never for your sister circle to become a therapy group, but you'd be surprised by the ways it might already be serving as a space that fosters healing and growth. I'd like to show you how we can further nurture this space as such.

THE POWER (AND PETTY?) OF GROUPS

I love my therapist. I wouldn't trade the experience of individual therapy for the world. But sometimes I feel like too much time has gone by before our next session. And honestly, I would love to get the opinion of multiple people about some of the less traumatic things that come up. It's one thing to have my therapist break down what's going on for me when I'm figuring out big issues but sometimes I would love to know that there are other people going through some of the more trivial things I go through. You know, the real petty stuff I think and feel and hope that other people might cosign also. Maybe that's not right but, hey, it's the truth.

−Kay, 27

Not Kay tapping in for the petty cosign! Yes, there is space in therapy to bring all of you, even the petty parts. Even though this gives me a hearty chuckle, what Kay is asking for is actually one of the reasons group therapy is so attractive: the idea that we could go somewhere and know that we are not alone in what we feel and that we won't be made to feel ashamed about it. In chapter 1, I shared the corrective emotional experience Jessica was able to have after I responded to her less critically than she expected following a missed session. While it is never too late for a corrective emotional experience, it is likely it would have happened far sooner had Jessica been participating in group therapy. In individual therapy there is only one other data point, one other person to offer the kind of reshaping of thought and perception that's needed, but within the group, with our sisters, multiple views exist. In a group, it's likely that Jessica's feelings of not being "good enough" would have been activated by a member's response to her, or she would have seen another member struggling in a similar way. This would then offer her an opening to share about her own experiences. The dynamics of healing in community are powerful and I think it is important to highlight them, as we've already discussed how critical our sister circles are to our lives. It goes back to our ancestral lineage, to the ways in which many of our foremothers lived communally. In order for our circles to indeed be spaces where healing happens, we must know more about *how* healing happens in groups and how we can create it.

As briefly mentioned in the introduction, Dr. Irvin Yalom has written extensively about the factors that lead to healing in groups. Originally published in 1970 and now in its sixth edition, *The Theory and Practice of Group Psychotherapy* outlines the eleven factors that invoke healing in a group:[1] universality, altruism, catharsis, imparting of information, development of socializing techniques, imitative behaviors, group cohesiveness, instillation of hope, interpersonal learning, corrective recapitulation of the primary family, and existential factors. I'll share more detail about each of these in a minute, but as is the case with many therapeutic offerings, it's important to note that people of color and Black women specifically did not make up the majority of the sample when this scholarship was produced. While these factors are relevant and do emerge in our particular group experiences, my work has also shown me that the presence of additional factors—humor, serving as possibility models, intuitiveness, and rhythm—aids in the healing of Black women's spaces. I'll share more about these as well.

Yalom's Curative Factors

Universality is the idea that we are all more alike than we are different. Though the content of our stories may vary, the feelings we experience are strikingly similar. You may not know what it's like to experience grief as it relates to the loss of a parent, but you probably know what it feels like to not have things work out as planned or to grieve the loss of a job or an opportunity. Underneath the content or the story we tell are the bare emotions of fear, sorrow, grief, anger, joy, and love that are the same for all of us. What happens in your own circle when you find out that one of your friends didn't get a promotion she really wanted?

Shoot, I'm probably crying more than she is.

Exactly. Before you even talk to her, you've likely already started imagining how she might be feeling and how you may need to show up for her. This is because you are probably able to relate to the feeling of being passed over for something that you really wanted and know how it stings. The pain we experience following any event is made more intense when we believe that no one else knows what it's like. Being able to show those in our circle that we get it, that we see them, helps to lessen this burden.

Altruism is central to healing in community and in many ways is at the heart of community. Altruism refers to the willingness to be of service to others without regard for what you may receive. For most of us, it feels good to be of service to another. In fact, the functioning of our formal and informal groups often relies on every party wanting to be helpful to the others. When we are drawn to being in circles with other people, there's usually something we feel we're going to get out of it, but also something we feel we can contribute. Part of our socialization as Black women definitely facilitates this. We are often taught that being of service to others is a positive attribute to possess, and this lesson usually works powerfully and positively within a sister circle where we know we can lean on one another. However, because of our socialization I do think we should also be mindful of boundary-setting around altruism, as many of us are already predisposed to losing ourselves in the service of others. If you're always volunteering to serve, or you're always the first one to show up when something happens, even when it's not truly feasible for you to do so, there may be room for you to strengthen a few of your boundaries so that you do not overextend yourself. There's a time to step up, Sis, but there's also a time to stand down.

Catharsis might be the easiest of all these concepts to wrap our minds around. It's that good feeling, that pleasure we get when we're finally able to share something that's been weighing on us. It's that moment in the group, formal or informal, when you say "the thing" and nobody runs away from you. While it is important and feels monumental to finally be able to share the secret that has felt so heavy, Yalom does comment that catharsis is more impactful in the later stages of a group. For example, sharing a secret you've been holding for a very long time to a group of your sisterfriends whom you've known for fifteen years is probably more impactful than sharing that same secret with a group of strangers. Many queer women talk about the feelings of joy that wash over them when they finally come out to friends and they are met with love and acceptance. In any instance, while we might be relieved if neither group ostracizes or shames us for the stories we share, having this happen in the confines of a relationship that has been meaningful to us for some time likely has a longer-lasting impact.

Imparting of information is another way that groups facilitate healing. We often enter into relationships in part because we want to be useful to others. We all know things based on our training and life experiences that can be helpful to others, and it's within the group that we can share those things to uplift and empower our sisters. We've seen this when veteran moms give a newer mom helpful tips on how to comfort a newborn with colic or ways to get a toddler to eat more veggies. This is essentially a huge part of the mission of Therapy for Black Girls: Black women referring Black women to Black women therapists, and Black women sharing resources and information to help one another along this path called life. As with all groups, there's always a chance of conflict and breakdown in circles where there is some imparting of information. A veteran mom's answer to a first-time mom's questions about discipline might be "Beat 'em," and if the new mom is looking to take the route of conscious or gentle parenting then there is room for offense. Because of this, there is also a need within the group for balance. Nobody likes the know-it-all in the group. There is a way to impart information so that people can take what they need and leave the rest without the group imploding.

One of the easiest routes to achieving this is by asking for permission before sharing a tip you believe will be helpful. Even though your intentions may be good, I am sure you can relate to the feeling of repeatedly being offered advice you didn't ask for. It doesn't typically feel great. To avoid this feeling for a sister in your circle, start by asking if she'd like the advice or whether there's another way you can support her.

Yalom also presents the development of our socializing techniques as a factor—how we learn to be in community with others in real time. We can get feedback about how we come across to others that will be helpful when we try to engage in other relationships. This is probably better demonstrated in a therapeutic context, but there are opportunities even in our informal sisterhoods to get trustworthy analysis of our personalities. This is especially true for Black women who, historically, have not been able to trust the assessments of other people because they are often rooted in stereotypes and assumptions about who we are as Black people and women. Remember when your homegirl told you that sometimes you don't look people in the eye and maybe that's why your job interviews haven't gone well? Who else can share something like that with you and have it come from a pure place of wanting you to win, not to tear you down?

Groups also allow us to practice imitative behaviors. They give us the opportunity to "try on" behaviors that we notice about others. For example, if there's someone in your sister circle who you observe to be assertive, there may be aspects of their behavior you desire to "try on" to see if they fit for you. Maybe that's speaking up first in a conversation or letting someone know that you don't agree with something they've said. Many of us have seen the sister circles that spend so much time together that it is hard to tell who is who. That often happens because we are "borrowing" things like language, outlook, and perspective from one another to help us establish who we are both as a part of the group and outside of it.

The next factor that shows up in groups is the installation of hope. Being in a group allows you to borrow the hopefulness of others until your stash is restored. One of the phrases I often find myself uttering in sessions with my clients is "you can borrow my courage or faith in you until yours is a little stronger." Perhaps you've had the experience of a sisterfriend believing in you more than you believe in yourself. She knows you can start that business or go back to school and is constantly speaking to you with the confidence that you might lack in the moment. Or maybe *you're* that friend. The one who is always championing your girls and pushing them to go higher. Keep that up! Hope is also installed when we see fellow members who may have struggled in similar ways come out on the other side of their ordeal. Seeing this allows us to envision it for ourselves.

The group dynamic provides an excellent opportunity for interpersonal learning, to discover what it means to actually be in relationships with others. It is a chance to practice skills that aid in the success and health of relationships: for example, how to confront someone who has said something offensive or how to receive feedback if you're the one who has been offensive. This could come up when you are dating somebody whom your sister circle has told you to stop messing with, and you find yourself having to have a very difficult conversation about boundaries, including saying, "I know that you may not feel like this person is the best for me, but this is a decision I want to make." Being able and willing to assert yourself in those kinds of situations, even though it may be difficult when people you care about don't agree with you, further develops your relationship skills and can make for richer and more authentic friendships.

This next factor sounds more complicated than it actually is: corrective recapitulation of the primary family. In short, being in a group of peers mimics the very first group we were ever a part of, our family unit. Yep, we are back to origin stories again. Sorry, not sorry. If we are typically the outspoken, take-charge person in our families, it is likely we will assume this position in a group as well. However, in a group this dynamic goes a step further, because then you are forced to examine how you came to take on the role you did in your family and whether it's actually one that feels authentic to you and works for you. Groups can both affirm what has been healthy and restorative about our family units and provide an alternate experience for the parts that felt invalidating and harmful.

Because much of life exists around our relationships with others, groups give us an incredible opportunity to grapple with those big life topics like death, love, and loss. These concepts are also referred to as existential factors. In a therapy group, when the member you've been most attached to decides to leave, it will undoubtedly stir something within you that likely relates to your thoughts and feelings about loss, abandonment, etc. Well, this happens in our friendships too. Perhaps you've had the experience of your sister circle being disrupted when one of you experiences a major life change like marriage, having children, or moving away. This often activates unrealized feelings of loss and abandonment that we don't have the language or skills to navigate. When a best friend gets engaged and moves across the country, some sisters will wonder what it means for the relationship and feel enormous grief over the change. They will wonder how the relationship survives after such a dramatic shift. Being able to process these kinds of issues in real time—whether in a therapeutic group setting or within the friend group—is invaluable and can offer excellent insight into how we make meaning of our lives.

Head swimming yet? Don't worry, Sis. We'll unpack how to do all of this in the chapters to come. I got you.

CURATIVE FACTORS SPECIFIC TO BLACK WOMEN

I knew I couldn't credibly talk about the healing power of groups without covering Yalom's scholarship, but I also know that he developed these factors at a time when Black people were rarely, if ever, participating in therapy. So, when I decided to write this book expressly for Black women, I knew there would be some missing nuance specific to Black women if I focused solely on Yalom's factors simply because we were not part of his study. While some of what he presents is incredibly consistent with my observations, I think it's important for me to expand his work so that it's more of a fit for what happens within groups of Black women. As a result, I've come up with four additional curative factors that impact the way Black women heal in a group dynamic.

The first additional factor I would offer as evidence of the way Black people, and Black women in particular, heal in the group dynamic is humor. Even in difficult situations, we will get these jokes off, right? I've observed that when Black women gather and we're talking about something difficult, someone may make a joke to add some levity. We aren't necessarily running away from the emotions that have come up but are instead creating a space for the emotions to be approached in a way that may be less threatening. The nature of our joy as a form of resilience cannot be ignored. One look at Black Twitter during a time of collective sorrow and grief will tell you that often the way we make sense of a difficult experience is dependent on our ability to find joy in the midst of pain. There has been many a meme that offered me a bit of respite for my soul when the news cycle has been especially hard.

Some might argue that the use of humor as a response to a difficult experience is distancing, and I can't say they're completely wrong. But if you only see the jokes and laughter without the context, you're not capturing the whole picture. Humor can often act as a connecting point. If we can connect over a joke, I may be able to offer feedback that you otherwise might not have been able to hear. Perhaps the laughter allows our sisterfriends to drop their defenses just enough so that they actually believe you when you say you'll be there for them.

Another factor that offers healing for Black women in the sister circle is the idea that we are serving as possibility models for one another. This will feel a bit similar to Yalom's language around imitation—a phrasing that often has negative connotations within the Black community—but I like the concept of the possibility model better as it allows for the women within the group to see one another not as competition nor as one person "trying to copy" the next, but as a model for what is possible. This is especially critical as we often find ourselves having to navigate systems of white supremacy and patriarchy that attempt to pit us against one another. However, in our sister circles, our healing spaces, we can look around and see other options and find ourselves saying, "Wow, I never considered that."

A great example of this came up in a recent Three for Thursday gathering. We were discussing how we might reimagine what romantic relationships look like, and a sister shared that her family owned a brownstone somewhere in New York and she and her husband have separate apartments in the building that are connected by a shared living room. Many of the women were shocked and curious. For some, it felt like a window of possibility opening up because, for them, that was an ideal living arrangement. I have my own space, you have yours, and we can hang out in the living room for our together time. I can go be as messy as I want in my space, and you can do what you want too. No fighting. The energy and conversation generated by that sister sharing that one part of her life opened up options and possibilities that many of us in the group hadn't considered feasible in light of the societal and cultural norms we feel pressed to abide by.

If I'm honest, it was a bit of a challenge to come up with language for intuitiveness, the next curative factor for Black women within the group. This concept, what we sometimes call "reading the room," is another one of those things that occurs within the sister circle that feels spiritual, or at the very least, intangible. Maybe it's part of our magic? I've often observed in groups of Black women the presence of individuals who can sense what's not being said. In essence, they know how to read the room and are able to keep the flow of engagement going by interjecting this added knowledge in subtle ways. In every sister circle, there are two conversations happening: the obvious one with sounds and actual words, and the nonverbal one that goes down in very embodied ways. The "cutting" of the eyes, the shrugging of shoulders, the leaning in or out . . . it's truly a rhythmic expression, like a dance, likely refined by our historical situations (see: colonization, enslavement, oppression) where we had to be very good at reading people and anticipating what would happen next, as our lives and livelihoods depended on it.

Having sisters who can read the room as a part of the circle adds a beautiful layer of depth to interactions as it often forces the conversation to be more in the here and now rather than the there and then. Sisters often marvel at others who are able to call out the elephant in the room in ways that are impactful but not abrasive. It has also been my experience that this intuitiveness creates space in groups of Black women for sisters who present in many different ways. Space is made for sisters who are a little more shy or who have difficulties with expression due to neurodivergence or who have previously not felt as comfortable in spaces full of other Black women. Everyone is afforded an opportunity to be seen and heard in the ways that are most comfortable for them.

The final factor is one that I've already hinted about here: rhythm. Within the sister circle, there is a cadence to our laughs that directs the flow of the conversation. We make room for a diversity of expression. Sis with the raucous, loud laugh somehow fits nicely with Sis who slaps her knee in silence. Their melodic demonstrations of joy are amplified by the movements of the sister who will literally run out of the room when something is funny. The energy is embodied and electric and kinetic and rides an undercurrent of joy and comradery that is not common in other groups.

The same goes with expressions of sorrow or rage in the group.

From a psychological perspective, when I'm observing or participating in a sister circle and I see these kinds of cultural expressions of emotions, I know that what I'm seeing is another form of safety. Within these groups, all of those expressions are seen as valid. By adding cadence and rhythm to the engagement, we are actually supporting the sisterhood. We are supporting us feeling good and, in turn, our bodies are healing. Something somatic is happening. Our central nervous systems are soothed and we physically expand in many ways. Some of our voices become louder. Some of us slide out of our chairs. Some of us feel like we can't breathe and yet we very much are breathing deep in all the ways that matter. This translates into taking up space in ways that we don't feel compelled or able to do in mixed company. So the distinct rhythm of Black women in the group dynamic creates safety and somatic healing.

As I've stated in pretty clear terms here, there is no denying that the foundations of psychology are normed on white cisgender men. In the eighties, four white women, Drs. Jean Baker Miller, Irene Stiver, Janet Surrey, and Judith Jordan, wrote a book, *Toward a New Psychology of Women,* that allowed us to learn more about the psychology of women and how our orientation to the world may be different. They wrote the book as a response to what they felt was a pathologizing of the way women tend to know and make meaning of themselves and the world. What has come of their work are frameworks like relational-cultural theory (RCT), which contends that women tend to gain greater self-knowledge through our relationships with others as opposed to attempts at autonomy. While many traditional psychological theories suggest that the "self" is the core construct to be studied, understood, and changed, relational-cultural theory suggests that connections are the sites of meaning and healing.

RCT posits that our growth as humans happens through connections with others that are based on mutual empathy and that these connections lead to zest, clarity, worth, creativity, and a desire for more connection.[2] When disconnections happen, as they do because we are human, growth can happen from our actively working through the disconnection. However, growth becomes difficult when we are not able to work through the disconnections that may occur in our relationships. An RCT lens views psychological health as the ability to continue to develop growth-fostering relationships with others and suggests that suffering is the result of repeated disconnections leading to isolation. Additionally, RCT suggests that it is through our relationships with other women that we heal past hurts. So, if this is the case, a solid argument can be made that the ideal healing environments for women are therapy groups and sister circles with other women. Author and professor emirita Joan Berzoff asks, "If we know that, for women, the self develops through relationships with other women, then why not set up therapeutic situations as close as possible to the naturally therapeutic network of women's adult friendships?"[3]

Given what we know about how Black women show up in the world, it is not a stretch to see why our relationships with each other are often where healing occurs. Author, professor, and feminist bell hooks often described sisterhood as resistance in her work. She wrote that when we find ourselves in situations where our humanity and dignity are constantly questioned, it is imperative that we create spaces where they are not.[4] But I've seen us take it a step further, where we are intentional about creating our spaces, not as a response to the white gaze, but as a place where we receive immense support. We gather and affirm one another.

The Covid-19 pandemic has served as probably the greatest call to support one another in my life and has presented countless opportunities for me to facilitate these kinds of spaces for sisters. In May 2020, I got a text from my friend Dr. Lakeysha "Key" Hallmon stating that she wanted to offer some type of support to the Black women who had been reaching out to her since the pandemic started. She shared that she had been getting calls from sisters struggling with anxiety, concerns about their businesses, and feelings of isolation. I had already been facilitating weekly virtual holding spaces for the TBG community to help with these same kinds of concerns. And as often happens when we talk, a grand scheme was developed. For sixteen weeks during the summer of 2020, at the height of both the global pandemic and the demonstrations of racial unrest as a result of police violence and brutality, Dr. Key, Dr. Ayanna Abrams, Dr. Joy Beckwith, and I began conducting virtual holding spaces for between 15 and 150 Black women to gather, share, and support one another during this time.

We called the group Anchored because we literally wanted the space to be something that could "hold Black women down" and give them a feeling of being tethered during such an uncertain and tough season. During one of the early sessions, a young sister shared that she had lost both of her parents when she was a child and, ever since, she had difficulty figuring out "adulting" activities like signing a lease for a car or choosing an insurance plan. She received a tremendous amount of support and advice from many of the other one hundred plus women on the chat that evening. Each week she returned and although she usually sat quiet during the sessions, she was always present. In our last session together, she shared through tears how much it had meant to her to be present every week even if she didn't share anything else. She said that each week she had learned something new that helped her to navigate life a little easier. Oh, and she was finally preparing to move into her first apartment. This is what healing in community does! It allows us to feel less alone, offers support in multiple areas, and teaches us more about ourselves in the context of relationship. Not only was Anchored a powerful experience for the participants, it was also a powerful experience for us as facilitators. We grew closer to one another through our preparation for the meetings and through our shared experience of holding space for the group, and what began as an effort to help turned into a lifeline for me throughout the pandemic.

These curative factors, Yalom's and mine, certainly contribute to healing in our groups, but there are a few other dynamics of groups I'd like to share that may also be helpful to us in strengthening our sister circles.

CONSISTENCY

Another factor that we should be mindful of in our sister circles is consistency. A group cannot achieve the level of cohesiveness it needs to be a supportive place for members if members do not consistently show up. As therapists, when we screen members before they join a group there is a significant amount of time spent discussing the importance of being present and on time for each group session. For members who are coming to the group with perhaps already shaky foundations with others in their lives, the group should be a stable and reliable space. During screening, if we find that members have previous engagements already scheduled that would lead them to miss group often, or if their schedule is not flexible enough to accommodate being there each week, we typically recommend that they either find another group that would work better for their schedule or wait until their schedule clears before joining. And if there is a reason that members must miss a session, they are encouraged to let the rest of the group know about it as soon as possible not only to demonstrate care for them, but also to cut down on the tendency some may have to create a story that is not accurate. Yes, it is that serious. Now, in our sister circles, of course, there isn't typically a screening process and we're not likely to ask someone to leave the circle because they can't make it to a Taco Tuesday, but I do believe it is in the best interest of our circles to consider what it means to be consistent in the space.

How might your circle look and feel different with everyone showing a similar level of commitment to showing up? I get it . . . schedules are hectic. We are often busy being caretakers, and life otherwise continues to life. In those instances, the first thing we tend to drop is time with our girls. But if our sister circles are the lifelines we often know them to be, it is important to treat them as such. While weekly get-togethers may not be available, I want you and your circle to think about what is possible. How active is the group chat? Are you marking important dates on your calendars so that you're less likely to forget someone's event? What plans are you all making to get together soon and how do you intend to protect that time?

SUBGROUPING

Raise your hand if this sounds familiar. You are in a group chat with the three other sisters in your circle, but you also have a chat with just you and two of those sisters in the circle who attend your church, and finally there is another group chat with the one sister from the circle you are closest with. I know I'm not the only one who finds themselves in this situation. In group therapy, this is called subgrouping, and while there are many reasons why subgrouping can be helpful, it's important to know that it can also introduce some challenges. In group therapy, subgrouping often happens when two or more members find themselves having lots in common, which sparks a desire to spend time with one another outside of the group. This can be beneficial to members as it often leaves them feeling less isolated and may serve as an additional source of support. Some therapeutic groups have strict rules about not subgrouping. Others are more flexible about it but do require that any contact with other members outside of the group be discussed in the following group session.

Now you may be thinking, "What is the problem with this?" Well, there really isn't an issue—until there is. Inevitably, something will come up in the subgroup that impacts what happens in the larger group. Perhaps the members end up experiencing a conflict that leaves one or more of them hesitant to return to the group or sister circle. Perhaps the members end up spending so much time together talking through concerns that they don't think that there is much left to talk about in the group and therefore begin to feel less committed. Or perhaps other members become jealous about the time the subgroup is spending together and it re-creates painful feelings of being rejected, therefore making the group space feel less safe and welcoming. All of these issues and more are possible and while they can be overcome, it's critical that we are mindful of them.

What does this mean for your sister circle? By no means am I telling you that everything has to stay in the main group chat. I know there are legitimate reasons why spin-off groups exist in our circles. I am asking you to consider what you might be missing about how this dynamic is impacting the larger unit. Is anyone feeling jealous or resentful because of relationships they are not a part of? Even if unintentionally, is someone's history of being rejected being re-created in the circle? Does it feel like there isn't a need to plan the yearly getaway because three of you already spend so much time together? And this is not to say that everyone is not entitled to have different types of relationships with each member of the circle; it's simply a call for you to think about how your circle may be subgrouping and what impact that could be having on individual members and the collective.

SPOTLIGHT-SEEKING

I'm not asking you to call anyone out, but does someone's name come to mind if I ask you who is the sister in your circle who must always be in the spotlight? Oh wait . . . is it you, Sis? So here's the thing: We all have our moments when we require a little more attention. Perhaps we're in the midst of a crisis and need more support, or we're celebrating something big and taking all opportunities to bask. But one member of a group monopolizing conversations and repeatedly requiring all the attention is a cause for concern. If this dynamic is happening in your circle, you're probably already aware of how it's impacting the group. What happens when the spotlight seeker starts talking at one of your get-togethers? It's likely someone is taking a deep breath, maybe another sister is subtly rolling her eyes, because both know it might be a while before anyone else gets to say anything. We often think we're being gracious by not calling out this behavior, but what we're actually doing is creating more distance between the spotlight seeker and the rest of the group by not letting the person know how this behavior impacts everyone else.

Spotlight-seeking can come from lots of different places. Sometimes it happens because seekers are anxious and worry that if they are not in the spotlight they'll be invisible in the group. Sometimes it's related to feeling like if they aren't always in crisis, their concerns won't be taken seriously. For many, it is based in some fear that the spotlight is what allows others to be connected to them. But as I've already described, constantly seeking the spotlight can actually turn people away. When seekers are in the midst of yet another story about the latest happenings, how long do you stay engaged? You may start making your grocery list in your head or thinking about the agenda for the meeting you need to plan at work later in the week. Your attention is not solely on them. You're probably not asking follow-up questions but instead just waiting for them to take a breath. This likely doesn't make you feel closer to them. Having spotlight seekers in your circle often results in feelings of resentment. Perhaps some sisters feel less excited about spending time together, or even worse, begin to exclude them from plans.

So, if there are sisters in your circle who are often in this role, the most beneficial thing someone in the circle can do is to make them aware of how their behavior is impacting the collective. I would not advise the entire group doing this all at once as it would likely be interpreted as a takedown, but I would suggest that one person be honest and say something like "It is a little awkward for me to share this, but I love you and think it's important for you to know that it often feels hard to stay connected to you when you're talking because you share a lot of information and don't always make space for others to share what's going on with them." This may be shocking for them to hear, especially if they're genuinely unaware of the dynamic, so give them some time to process what's been shared and be open to answer any follow-up questions they may have. It's important to reinforce that you don't want them to silence themselves completely, but simply to be more mindful about how everyone can have space to share, respond, and connect.

I NEED HELP, BUT NOT LIKE THAT

In group therapy, one type of member who often pops up is what is described as the help-rejecting complainer.[5] This is the person who frequently finds themselves in a crisis, often solicits a lot of feedback from the group, and then proceeds to either dismiss the feedback or not follow through with suggestions that have been offered. Are you able to recognize this pattern for anyone in your own circle? Do you or others find yourselves saying, "Girl, I ain't telling her nothing else. She's going to do what she wants to do anyway!" If so, it is very likely that this behavior leaves the rest of the circle feeling frustrated, confused, and maybe even helpless about how to respond to this sister. If you recall our discussion of attachment styles in chapter 1, people who exhibit help-rejecting complaining behaviors would likely have an attachment style that is highly anxious and avoidant.[6] They are often simultaneously desperate for connections with others and also uncomfortable with the need to rely on others. In your sister circle, it may be a very delicate balance of trying to show support for this person while also setting boundaries around your energy and time in order to not become burned out by trying to show up for her. If someone in your circle displays this behavior, here are a few things that may be helpful to you:

1. Try to engage with your sympathy for how they might be feeling: how hard it must feel to want help but at the same time be afraid that no one will help or that the help won't be effective. I'm not saying this will be easy, especially if you're already feeling frustrated, but it's worth trying.

2. Limit the amount of advice or feedback you offer. It doesn't feel good to continue to offer suggestions to someone only for them to tell you why it won't work. Instead of continuing to offer solutions, try instead to offer empathy for what they're experiencing. You can try saying something like "Wow, I'm so sorry that happened. It sounds frustrating" or "Ugh, I hate that you're going through this. I hope you're able to find a solution that works for you soon."

3. Encourage them to talk through their own plan for solving the issue. To avoid getting trapped in the endless loop of giving a suggestion and having it rejected, instead encourage them to develop a plan for how they're going to tackle whatever the problem is. As a continuation to the previous suggestion, you might say something like "I hope you're able to find a solution that works for you soon. I'm happy to hear some things you're considering to take care of this issue. I've got fifteen minutes before my next meeting."

As you can see, there are plenty of ways in which knowing more about group dynamics can help to strengthen our sister circles. And when we strengthen our sister circles, we strengthen how Black women show up as a collective in the larger world.

QUESTIONS FOR REFLECTION

1. Which of Yalom's curative factors resonate with you? Can you think of ways that you might incorporate some of the other factors into how you navigate your sister circle?

2. What characteristics of sisters in your circle have you found yourself "trying on"? Was it a good fit? What did you learn about yourself from the experience of trying it on?

3. Are there subgroups within your circle? How are these managed? How does the larger group feel about the subgroups?

CHAPTER 3

I Am My Sister's Keeper and She Is Mine

In the comfort of daily conversations, through serious conversation and humor, African-American women as sisters and friends affirm one another's humanity, specialness, and right to exist.

–Patricia Hill Collins

When I first read the ice cream shop Facebook post I shared at the opening of the book, I was struck by how succinctly and vividly it captured what I believe is the true essence of sisterhood. The instinct that "Supa Sista" had to step in and make sure that baby girl was cared for is emblematic of the world Black women create with and for one another. It is the same instinct that shows up when a sister tucks that tag in on the back of our dress, or when the sister in front of you at the grocery store comes up a little short and you offer to add her items to your own tab. It's the same instinct that compels you to stick around after a sister has finished her presentation at a conference to let her know that she crushed it. This instinct is critical to our healing, and it must be nurtured. When I say sisterhood heals, I mean that we heal individually within the confines of our relationships with one another, we heal together within the confines of our sister circles, and the healing on these levels leads to our collective healing. When I am well, I can treat others well. When we are well, our communities thrive.

ALL MY SISTERS

I've been called "judgy" by friends and family and, yes, maybe there's some truth to that. Whenever I see sisters, especially the ones I don't know like celebrities and high-profile people, doing things I don't agree with, I tend to make my feelings known. And truthfully, I've never thought of that as a bad thing. I think I just have high standards for how Black women should show up in the world, especially when so much is stacked against us. But I'm also learning that my standards aren't the baseline for everyone. And, if I'm really honest, I'm beginning to see that there is absolutely a direct connection between how I see and deal with sisters I don't know and the conflicts I'm currently having with the sister-friends I love dearly. I want to do better at seeing all my sisters . . . and ultimately myself . . . in a more positive light.

—Christine, 32

I'm so glad Christine landed on this revelation. Think of it like this: Our sister circles sit in the context of a larger sister circle (work, school, church, sorority), which sits in a larger circle (neighborhood, city, industry, interest), which sits in an even larger circle (country, world, diaspora). Much has been studied and written about the sense of collectivism that is often central to the lives of African Americans. Collectivism refers to the tendency to put the needs of others in the group before your own. This tendency often shows up in the sense of obligation many have to community uplift, to leaving something better than we found it, and to ensuring the longevity of our community. Because our ancestors believed in the connection of all things, this sense of collectivism is often thought to be historical, and it has evolved with our legacy in this country. Our fictive kinship relationships, the idea that there is some obligation to one another even though we are not related by blood, are a modern-day example, like the way we refer to one another as sisters, which I use throughout the book.

A collectivist sensibility depends on us having a very expansive notion of what it means to be a sister. Perhaps we can dig into this now. What does it mean to you to be a sister to someone? For me, it is indicative of a chosen, intentional, and purposeful connection. With those in our sister circles, it implies a greater sense of intimacy and voluntary obligation to and for one another. In the greater collective, it implies a seeing and a knowing that reside outside of a more formal relationship but one that is familiar all the same. If we choose to be sisters, what is our responsibility to one another? I believe the responsibility lies in two areas: seeing one another and supporting one another.

SEEING ONE ANOTHER

When I ask sisters what makes their relationships with other Black women so special, something I often hear is that "they really see me." In a world that often overlooks our talents and contributions and where we can be made to feel invisible, it is invaluable to inhabit spaces where we are truly seen. What does this look like in practice, and how can we make sure we are really seeing one another?

We hear tales of others not moving out of our way on sidewalks when they are walking toward us, as if we are not there. We know what happens in medical settings where our pain is not believed and our reports of what we are experiencing are second-guessed. Serena Williams famously shared how she had to repeatedly advocate for herself shortly after giving birth so that her concerns about blood clots were taken seriously. We know these stories and we also know the release of tension that happens when our physician walks in and it's another Black woman, or we share a knowing glance with one another when someone makes an offhand comment that everyone else seems to miss. There is power in seeing one another so that we do not find ourselves alone and isolated and questioning whether something actually happened the way we know it did. In an effort to continue to see one another I suggest we do a few things:

1. Be on the lookout for other Black women in our surroundings and acknowledge them with a quick hello or brief conversation.

2. Compliment a Black woman we see in public.

3. Be watchful of younger sisters in our spaces.

SUPPORTING ONE ANOTHER BY LIFTING AS WE CLIMB

The truth is, many Black women feel some kind of responsibility to serve, support, or, at a basic level, look out for other sisters, whether we know them or not. This is a prime example of how the global sisterhood functions. It's not just about hooking our girl up with an interview because we've known her forever. It's also about seeing a sister in need "out there" and figuring out how to swoop in and help. In the article "Giving Back to the Community: How African Americans Envision Utilizing Their PhD," Associate Professor of Leadership and Counseling at Eastern Michigan University Dr. Carmen McCallum explored the collectivist orientation I discussed earlier. She found that a majority of African Americans in the study felt a responsibility to give back to their community as a driving force for getting a PhD.[1] Sisterhood is largely based on this idea of being responsible to the sisters around us and those coming behind us.

Much research has discussed the importance of mentoring for Black women, especially when the mentors are other Black women. Black women tend to climb the corporate ladder at lower rates and are often largely absent from the C-suite. Much has been written about how difficult it is for Black women academicians to obtain tenure and how they often find themselves in a hostile environment without the presence of other supportive Black women. However, if they are able to find support from other Black women early on, they tend to thrive. A study conducted by sociologists

Nicole Brown and Ruby Mendenhall revealed that mentoring relationships between Black women make the academy "more accessible, supportive, and beneficial for Black women."[2]

WE ALL WE GOT

We know the statistics. On average, Black women are paid 42 percent less than white men and 21 percent less than white women.[3] Black women are more likely to die in childbirth than their counterparts. In 2020, Black women and girls accounted for 14 percent of the U.S. population yet made up 31 percent of the women and girls killed by men and boys in single victim/single offender incidents.[4] Black women are the fastest growing demographic of entrepreneurs yet raise the lowest amounts of capital for their businesses. It is not a secret that much of the world and life is not set up for Black women to succeed and thrive. So when we say "We all we got," it's not hyperbole. For years, it has been clear that we are the ones who help our sisters succeed, thrive, and stay safe. And, yes, many of us are also making efforts to change and/or abolish the systems that have harmed us in the first place, but we recognize that this is not enough and that we cannot rely on the slow pace of systemic change to ensure our livelihoods, so we do what we must.

There's actually a name for the ways we navigate these systems and, in turn, provide communal support to one another: healthy cultural paranoia. Because Black women often have a shared history of trauma—the fact that many of us are acutely aware of the ways in which systemic obstacles exist to block us from surviving and thriving—we are rightfully a little paranoid about trusting those same systems to solely care for us. We see this in action when we walk into a room and catch the eye of our sister in a way that says, "If something pops off in here, I got you." It's likely the impetus for actress and producer Issa Rae's declaration on an awards show red carpet that she's rooting for everybody Black—reminiscent of how our aunties and grandmas would root extra hard for the Black contestant on *Wheel of Fortune* or *The Price Is*

Right. Black women are too often seen as the underdog no matter the scenario and so we tend to feel compelled to hold one another down. Our sisters' dreams—and their fulfillment—in many ways become our own.

Black women are big dreamers, and the beauty of our dreams is that they are so expansive: They are about not only how our individual lives might be different but how the world might be different. One of my favorite questions to ask Black women is "If money were no object, what would you create in the world?" I am often deeply moved by the answers. Something I've noticed recently is that there is a theme to the responses. On more than one occasion I've gotten a sister talking about building a commune big enough for entire families and friend groups to come together to live and play. A variation of this has been about occupying farmland that is ripe for nourishment but also provides a space for sisters to frolic and be free. I am not surprised that a theme of community and togetherness is present when I ask sisters this question. It feels consistent with what I know and observe of us. It aligns with this idea that *we* must be the ones to protect us. That said, if our dreams for the world involve a community where we are responsible to and for one another in large and small ways, what kinds of guidelines and conversations might we need to have to make it so?

THE SPOKEN AND UNSPOKEN GUIDELINES OF THE GLOBAL SISTERHOOD

I've often believed that there are some spoken and unspoken guidelines of sisterhood that are the foundation of healthy relationships, whether we are talking about two besties who grew up together, the sister circle that supports us through every season, or the acquaintances or sisters we don't know intimately but feel a responsibility for at a soul level. When I facilitate groups and workshops for sisters, I often begin by engaging them in the process of setting some guidelines to govern our time together. I typically share about things like confidentiality, the importance of pacing yourself when sharing, and being able to ask questions even if you think everyone else already knows the answer. I then invite them to share the things that are important to them to make the space as welcoming and safe as possible for everyone. I wonder if we might do that now. I have a few thoughts about some guidelines that I believe can help as we continue to nurture our collective sisterhood, but I also invite you to share your thoughts here as well.

Be One Another's Soft Place to Land

It's within the context of relationships where we are often able to confront the parts of ourselves we'd rather not face. This is typically called shadow work. We are more inclined to entrust the pieces of ourselves that we usually don't want other people to see, that we don't want to see ourselves, to another sister—especially in light of the systemic oppression we are bound to face. Patricia Hill Collins also explores this in *Black Feminist Thought*: "For African-American women, the listener most able to pierce the invisibility created by Black women's objectification is another Black woman. This process of trusting one another can seem dangerous because only Black women know what it means to be Black women. But if we will not listen to one another, then who will?"[5] That's hard, right? And all parties would benefit from some healthy self-compassion so that we can provide a safe place for one another to lay our burdens down.

I'm reminded of all the times I've seen a Black child upset at the airport or in some other public place and the mom is struggling to calm them. It's almost instinctual that I will dig into my purse and find one of my kids' toys or a pack of fruit snacks to help out. As a parent, and a Black mom in particular, I'm well acquainted with the anxiety and embarrassment we feel when our child is "cutting up in public," especially since we know that our children are not seen in the same light as white or other non-Black children. And, yes, while I might acknowledge a general solidarity with any mother going through that, I feel a specific sense of responsibility to ease the tension of my sister, to not judge her or her child but to take action to be her "soft place to land" as she's trying to navigate a hard time.

Assume the Best Intentions

We've all had those moments when a difficult interaction occurs in part because we made assumptions about a sister beforehand. Especially in light of the events of the past few years, many of us are on edge. Instead of popping off, we should ask ourselves what it looks like to enter a situation with the mindset "I'm sure this sister is doing the best that she can in this moment."

Understanding the basics of how we have learned (or not learned) to connect provides the basis for how we find ourselves navigating our friendships. It's the foundation of it. I know that I am not alone in feeling that in many ways all we have is one another, so if this is the case, it behooves us to do the very best we can to build the strongest, most gracious, most affirming relationships with one another. The first step in doing this is evaluating the assumptions we have about one another.

Let's say you're attending a conference in your field, and you walk into a breakout session and see one other sister sitting there in a sea of non-Black people. How are you inclined to react?

"Hey, girl, hey!"

"Nope. I'm not going to be obvious and sit next to the only other Black girl in the room."

"Ooooh, I know we are going to have so much in common!"

"She's probably one of them types that don't want to be bothered with her people."

Head nod.

Our responses in this scenario are very telling. Would you be the one to immediately get excited and attempt to sit next to her and offer some version of the "Yasss, Sis. I see you." Or would you try not to sit next to her because that kind of familiarity feels deeply uncomfortable? Or would you simply notice her as another person in the room and take the first seat available? To be clear, this is not some kind of wayward litmus test. It's just an exercise in examining what comes up for you as you think about how you might behave and then what story you are telling yourself about what is happening in the moment. There is no right or wrong response, but here are a few thoughts that come up for me.

In this scenario, I am most likely going to try to sit next to her and offer some version of "Hey, girl, hey!" I'd probably be excited about not being the "only one" in a space and would feel a sense of comradery with the other Black woman there, even if it's only brief. If the presenter says something racist, or someone in the audience asks a question that goes off the rails, I would look forward to sharing knowing glances or even backing each other up, if necessary. Do you see how I built a whole story in my head about this interaction with a completely fictional sister? I assumed she would be open to my "Hey, girl." Everything I conjured up about how we might interact with each other going forward at the conference is based on my previous, mostly positive experiences with Black women in a professional environment. But let's say you're not inclined to sit next to her. Why might that be?

Perhaps you lean more toward the introversion side of the personality spectrum and you're already feeling peopled out. Perhaps you are hyperaware that you and she are the only two Black people in the room, and you know that when we "sit together at the lunch table" certain connotations are created. Maybe sisters have burned you in the past so you would just rather not engage. Perhaps you fall into the camp of not thinking much about her at all and you just want to sit wherever a seat is available. Again, none of these responses are wrong, but they are rooted in something. An experience. A narrative. I'd just like you to think about what may be driving your behavior. And then I want you to think about how you might respond if you are the sister who's already seated, and another Black woman walks into the room. Would you expect or want her to sit next to you? Would you prefer she didn't, or would you not care either way? Does that change anything for you? Do you expect others to do more or less than you would do yourself? What changed, if anything?

I'm asking you to play with these scenarios in your head because I don't think we always realize how our assumptions about others take shape in how we interact with them, particularly other Black women. Let's say that you are the sister who's already seated in the conference room and the second sister walks in. If she doesn't sit next to you and you are feeling some kind of way about that, it's important to ask yourself what's happening for you in that moment. What story are you telling yourself about why she didn't sit next to you? Do you think she's a little shy, or have you immediately turned her into a villain? Would your story change if you saw her at lunch enthralled in a conversation with a table of white women? What about if you saw her sitting by herself at lunch? Each new piece of information can alter our perception and thereby challenge our assumptions. I'd like to gently remind you that we rarely have a complete story when we encounter someone for the first time. Let's offer one another the benefit of the doubt.

Extend Grace and Compassion to One Another and Ourselves

In those instances where we have chosen to assume the best of intentions and it still results in a sister showing up in a way that is challenging, we can still extend grace and compassion to her because we don't yet know what's going on in the background. We can never go wrong with leading with kindness. This is especially true in our interactions with our sisters who are service workers. Yes, your plane is late and your gate agent has not been that forthcoming. Sure, your impatience might be driving you to cuss the girl out but, Sis, who does that really serve? Off-loading your pain might feel good for a second but it won't make your plane arrive any faster. And the truth is, you don't know what's going on in that sister's life. Extending some compassion to her for what is sometimes a thankless job will go a long way. As the elders say, "You catch more flies with honey than vinegar." We should have more empathy for our sisters, *especially* if we are aware of the systems at play on these jobs because we have to battle those same systems on our own. Plus, we might have been the seventieth person to ask Sis that same question, and we know good and well that asking a sister something more than twice will garner a side-eye, at the very least.

Share Your Story So That Others Feel Safe to Share Theirs

The world of tennis showcased a really great example of this type of sharing when four-time Grand Slam singles champion Naomi Osaka decided to choose her own mental health over the sport she loved, which likely empowered Olympic gold medalist Simone Biles to do the same thing in 2021 during the Summer Games in Tokyo. After Megan Thee Stallion began sharing her experiences with grief and domestic violence, many sisters began offering her support and sharing their own stories. Even Congresswoman Ayanna Pressley's candid conversation about her journey with alopecia, a skin condition that causes hair to fall out, seemed to open the floodgates for other sisters to discuss their own experiences surrounding the loss of their hair. The entire thesis of the #MeToo movement, founded by Tarana Burke, is based on this idea that sharing one's story, in this case of sexual assault, abuse, or harassment, frees another woman to share her own. The bottom line? There's something incredibly liberating in sharing our stories—for ourselves and for our sisters.

In Service to All My Sisters

Black women have had to develop our sisterhoods for survival, without a doubt. But our sisterhoods are also born out of our common interests and experiences. And more than anything, our sisterfriendships offer us a pleasure we can't readily find elsewhere.

The universal experience of being Black women—the altruism of serving one another in trials and triumphs, the catharsis of sharing your heart—is by definition what drives the global sisterhood. It's what compelled Supa Sista to help out that young angel in the ice cream line. My experience in my own personal friendships was a significant part of what led me to start Therapy for

Black Girls. Sisterhood is what allows us to take off our masks. In our sister circles, we can figuratively take off our bras and not have to be "on" like the rest of the world requires. We can be great, but we can also be mediocre. We can be full of joy and also be holding grief from a devastating loss. Both/and. We can separate ourselves from the heavy cloak of Black excellence when it has been our sole identity for too long. That safety then allows us to show up in the world refreshed and ready to be all we were meant to be. It allows us to show up for each other in ways the world chooses not to. Audre Lorde wrote, "Without community, there is no liberation."[6] It's freedom that these formal and informal groups afford us and that allows us to help others get free. Our sisterfriendships are the relationships we choose. It's the place where we can experience radical softness, intentionality, and care simply because we are.

EXERCISE FOR REFLECTION

Let's try an exercise that will illuminate how connected our personal sister circles are to the collective: the global sisterhood. Take a moment to label the circles on the following page with the names of people, organizations, etc., that can be categorized as your sister circle, secondary circle, and collective circle.

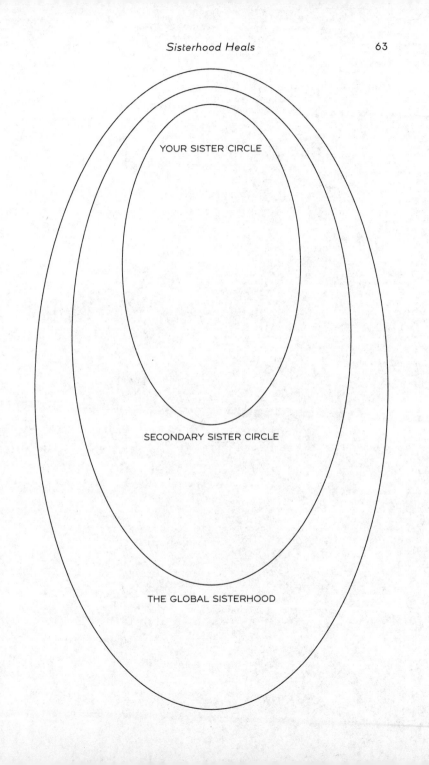

YOUR SISTER CIRCLE

SECONDARY SISTER CIRCLE

THE GLOBAL SISTERHOOD

PART II

Count on Me through Thick and Thin

She is a friend of my mind. She gather me, man.
The pieces I am, she gather them and give them back to
me in all the right order. It's good, you know, when you got
a woman who is a friend of your mind.

—Toni Morrison, Beloved

CHAPTER 4

The Load Is Lighter When We Help One Another Carry It

For Black women who are addicted to being controlling, asking for help can be a loving practice of surrender.

–bell hooks

On the *Therapy for Black Girls* podcast, the term "holding space" is something we talk about quite often. It's become a buzzword these days, but it's much more than jargon. Holding space refers to creating a figurative container for others to share openly and honestly. It is creating an environment that feels safe and supportive enough to share the whole story. When we hold space for a sister, we are putting ourselves to the side so that she has the floor—to be, to feel, to express herself in a "judgment-free zone"—no matter how complex, messy, or chaotic the circumstances may be.

ALONE IN A CROWD

I can't even begin to count the number of times I could be hanging with my girls, laughing and seemingly having a good time, yet I still feel so alone. I don't feel connected in the ways I used to. My friendship group has pretty much been the same since I was in high school, and back in the day, I always felt like I could bring anything to them and they would help me sort through things or at the very least support me. Nowadays, I'm not sure that's the case. It's not like they've said anything that makes me think that. It's just that my problems are bigger now and I get the sense that they aren't able to support me in the ways they used to. Not sure if it's me or them or both though.

—Tiana, 35

Let's talk about it! What Tiana is describing is not uncommon. I've heard many sisters make similar comments, and I want to take some time to dig into what I'm curious about based on what's shared time and time again. The first thing that comes to mind is, *I wonder if she's experiencing other depressive symptoms?* The disconnection and feelings of isolation described can sometimes be pieces of a larger puzzle, indicative of a depressive disorder that can definitely impact both our ability to hold space for others and our ability to be held. The other thing I wonder is, *What pieces of this story have been checked out or shared with Tiana's circle?* She's stated that her friends haven't said anything to make her believe they're not there to support her, yet she's also holding on to this idea that they can't be there for her. Trust me, Tiana is not the first sister to come up with an entire narrative about how others feel about her, but what I would encourage her (and you too if you've felt this way) to do is to share how she's feeling and let her sisters tell her what's actually happening.

If you're like Tiana, perhaps you've sensed a disconnect in your friendships that needs some attention, or maybe you've reacted to that distance by creating your own. Either way, you won't know until you say something. Finally, Tiana mentioned something that feels like a universal Black girl cry for help: "My problems are bigger now." I know many sisters are nodding their heads in recognition because they too have been guilty of feeling like their problems were too big to share or that sharing would burden others with their concerns. This is not an absolute fact, Sis. One thing I've seen more often than not in my work with Black women is that we want to be there for those in our circle but either don't know how or don't recognize that there's a need. I think you might be surprised by how your circle steps up if you share what's going on with you.

HOLDING SPACE FOR OTHERS

The sentiments shared by Tiana give us an excellent opportunity to dig deeper into what impacts our ability to hold space for others, what it means to allow others to hold space for us, and what this actually looks like in practice.

Many might think the first step in holding space for others is figuring out what to do or say, but it actually starts with a self-assessment. The first question you want to ask is "Do I have the capacity to hold space for the person?" If what we are hoping to do is to create a figurative container for others, we must ensure the container is not leaky or full of holes. Let's look at a few of the factors that might contribute to the leaks.

One of the reasons it can be difficult to hold space for others is that many of us are way overextended. In a world that demands we be everything in every space (our businesses, extended family, social calendar, etc.), we too often try to keep all the balls in the air at once. We attempt to do all the things and be all the things to everyone. Over the last decade, and certainly in the past three years, the complaint I've heard most often from Black women I've worked with is "I'm tired" or "I don't have the bandwidth for anything else." For many of us, and perhaps this is the case with Tiana's sisterfriends, there is no room, no margin, for anything other than what's going in our own lives because we are spread so thin. To put it bluntly, life be lifing, and sometimes there just isn't any more left to offer others.

When we are so wrapped up in whatever's happening in our own lives, it can be easy to forget to ask our sisters (especially the ones who seem the strongest, the ones who usually step in as caregivers) how they are doing or what they need during difficult times. Perhaps we overlook their pain after a breakup or even a bad day on the job with a quick "I'm sorry" without leaning in to listen, asking for more details, and making it clear that we really want to know. I suspect we all do this far more than we realize, or perhaps are ready to own up to. And here's the thing: There's no need to feel bad if you don't have it to give. It's more important for you to recognize when you're at capacity and show up in whatever ways you can. Perhaps all you can offer at the moment is exchanging memes via text or sending a DoorDash gift card. Don't discount how far that can go in letting someone know you care.

But let's not end this conversation on self-assessment without acknowledging our varying levels of capacity. It's important to stop for a moment and look at *why* we're so overextended and what we might be able to do to regain some bandwidth, not simply so it's available to support our circle, but also to allow ourselves some breathing room. For many of the sisters I've worked with, the overextension is related to one or a few things: societal expectations of being all things to all people, disproportionately connecting their work to their worth, using busyness to escape feelings, or a misguided belief that their only value comes from what they are able to offer others. Do any of these feel familiar to you? Which ones resonate the loudest? Would you take a moment to journal about the following questions to help get some clarity?

1. Where did these messages of having to be everything to everybody come from?

2. What keeps me invested in holding on to being all things to all people?

3. Who benefits most from my being overextended?

4. If I were less overextended, how might my life look different? What would I do? How would I feel? How would I know I was less overextended? Describe in as much detail as possible.

Another barrier that can make it difficult for us to hold space for our sisters is the fact that sometimes the things they need help carrying are heavy for us as well and may trigger our own "stuff" and impair our ability to be nonjudgmental. As therapists, we're trained to assess when our own issues are getting in the way of being able to create a nonjudgmental space for our clients to share. For example, if I am a therapist struggling with difficulties in my marriage and I have a client who is presenting with similar concerns in her marriage, it is important for me to be alert and mindful that my feelings about my own partner and relationship do not interfere with how I may be viewing my client's relationship with her partner.

However, many of our sisters don't have this training, so what ends up happening when we are asked to hold space for our girl is that our own stuff gets in the way. Our feelings about our partner can cloud what she is saying about hers. Our desire for our girl to be in a different place than she is on the job might interfere with what she is actually saying about the job. We might have intended to provide a space where she is able to talk openly about her concerns, but it has turned into a space where she doesn't feel comfortable and perhaps feels ashamed. Now listen, the goal is not to make you a therapist within your circles—even if you are a therapist, that would not be appropriate. The goal is to simply help you be mindful of how your stuff might be getting in the way of you showing up the way you'd like to for your sisters. Are you trying to figure out how to know if your own stuff is interfering with you being able to hold space for someone else? No worries, I got ya! Here are some questions to ask yourself:

1. Is the situation my sister is confiding in me about too much like one I've experienced in the past? Am I really listening to her or am I replaying my own situation?

2. What personal work have I done to move past a similar situation in my own life? How much time has passed since the situation was resolved?

3. How am I feeling about what she's sharing? Am I more angry/upset/hurt about it than she is?

BEING HELD

Sometimes the issue isn't about a sister's ability to hold space for us. Sometimes it's about our capacity to be held. We need a moment there, right? In all of our efforts to exude strength, keep it together, and keep all the balls in the air, we can consciously and subconsciously reject one of the very things that might just help us hold it together. In fact, there is evidence that those who subscribe to this Strong Black Woman (SBW) schema[1] that has had us in a chokehold for far too long might isolate themselves during periods of stress. Isn't that something? At times, we get so invested in seeming strong that we think it's wrong to even let anyone see us struggle.

Whenever I have clients who are struggling with removing their SBW capes and making room in their lives to receive the care they so readily give, I usually realize that they haven't actually figured out *how* to release some of the things they are carrying, nor do they know *what* to let go of. Often, "Why don't we take a look at everything you're doing?" I will ask. "Make a list of all your responsibilities. The things that are keeping you preoccupied and unable to be there for yourself and others." I encourage them to do an audit and look for things they can delegate or areas where they can ask for more help.

But I have to do it all, Dr. Joy! I don't want what someone else does on my behalf to reflect poorly on me!

No, you don't *have* to do it all. Try something else. If you really want to lay down your SBW cape, then you will first have to be willing to try something new. To do something that might be uncomfortable, but also might free you up to take better care of your soul and be more present for your friends. If it works, great! If it doesn't, then we try something else. The question then becomes, Are you really afraid that laying down your cape in this way won't work—or that it actually will?

Sis, I officially give you permission to fall apart if you must. You have permission to not do or be everything. To "get somebody else to do it," as the popular TikTok audio says. It's not wrong. It's okay to not be strong. Actually, being vulnerable is more of an indication of true strength than wearing a mask of toughness.

When was the last time you had a hug from someone that allowed you to completely melt? You know what kind of hug I mean. The kind you get from the people you love after you've been trying unsuccessfully to hold it together for far too long. No words even have to be spoken. The safety, comfort, and security they engender and represent let you know that all is right with the world, even if just for that moment. Your shoulders drop, your heart rate slows, and maybe a few tears start to fall. Hugs are a physical manifestation of space being held for us, but our sisters holding space for us emotionally can conjure this same calming effect. What makes both of these experiences so powerful, what truly allows us to be held, is our ability to lean into vulnerability.

Being vulnerable is the process of sharing ourselves and the truths about who we are and our experiences even if we're not sure they will be accepted. It is the practice of sharing the things we'd rather keep locked away for fear we'll be judged by others. Vulnerability is an important part of our humanity because it is the only pathway to the affirmation and connection so many of us deeply crave. But the affirmation and connection we receive will always ring hollow if it is based on the character we've created for the world as opposed to who we really are, flaws and all.

The upsides to vulnerability sound glorious but let us not be fooled into thinking it's always easy. It's the equivalent of being emotionally naked and, especially for Black women, not easy at all sometimes. The ways we have been socialized to perform strength often make it difficult for us to tap into and offer vulnerability, frequently to our own detriment. The Strong Black Woman schema I mentioned earlier is, in many ways, a protective posture against racism, sexism, and all the other isms and may offer us the illusion of control. But it may also keep us from identifying and articulating what we need and reaching out for help. One theory that explains the impact this has on us is the self-silencing theory, first posited by psychologists Drs. Dana Jack and Diana Dill.[2] Self-silencing theory suggests that women bite their tongues due to a loss of self in a relationship or fear of one's authentic self, rejection, loss, and/or alienation. Self-silencing manifests in four distinct behaviors: (1) silencing the self (i.e., women not directly asking for what they want or telling others how they feel), (2) divided self (i.e., women presenting a submissive exterior to the public despite feeling hostility and anger), (3) care as self-sacrifice (i.e., women putting the needs and emotions of others ahead of their own), and (4) externalized self-perceptions (i.e., women evaluating themselves based on external [cultural] standards).[3]

Vulnerability can also be a challenge if we don't have a great history of our wounds being tended to with care. Perhaps we shared something we thought would be in confidence and it was, instead, broadcast widely. Or maybe we divulged something that was painful and got ridiculed. Each encounter we've had like this makes it a little more difficult to lay bare ourselves with one another. The possibility of rebuilding this space is certainly there, but it's challenging to overcome that kind of diminishing of one's confidence. On the flip side, what an exhilarating and tender feeling it is to share something we've been holding for so long and be met with support and encouragement. This is the both/and of vulnerability. It is both difficult and rewarding.

Because so much of our socialization involves being taught to be disconnected from our inner experiences, it can also be harder for us to tap into our vulnerability. "Little girls don't say things like that," "you're overreacting," and "you're strong, you got this" are just a few examples of phrases thrown at us that often lead us to believe that we cannot trust our inner knowing. We start to believe that perhaps what we're experiencing is not accurate and someone else knows better than we do. For too many of us, our interior lives end up on the back burner because the breadth and depth of emotions that others are allowed to feel seem to be off-limits to us.

Finally, in order for us to allow ourselves to be held we must be aware of what I call the paradox of the rock. This refers to the tendency for the strong ones, the caretakers, the "everything's fine, I'm fine" ones in our circle to be largely overlooked and not offered care because of the false assumption that they must be okay because they appear so. I mean, brick houses don't crumble, right? Research suggests that the repeated tendency of some Black women to display strength in the face of physical and emotional hardship can lead to a host of concerns, including psychological distress like depression, anxiety, and disordered eating.[4] So, yes, the rocks are often the ones who appear strong and put together. They are usually trying to hold it all together for everyone else. But they also can be the ones who are internally shattering. In fact, those of us in community with sisters who are rocks often know that it's a façade. We're easily deceived by their strength because they appear engaged and don't show any outward signs of strain. But if we slow things down even a little bit and scratch off that top layer, the truth bubbles to the surface.

If you are the rock in your circle, I want you to take some time to explore what's driving this role for you. Where did you learn that it was not okay for you to have needs and wants like everyone else? What might it look like to actually ask for help or have your needs met? Many times it is the asking for help that makes it difficult for us to be held. We assume others should just know that we're struggling. We show up for others; why don't they show up for us? This is the paradox. It may not be that they don't want to show up for us—they just don't know that we need it. The rock's pain is not readily seen on the surface. I understand how this can be frustrating if you're someone who expends a lot of energy taking care of others, but I also want you to consider what's more important for you: to receive assistance and support or to be offered help before you ask for it.

Rock Revisions: An Exercise

We've already discussed that one of the most difficult things for those who are the "rocks" in their group to do is to ask for help. If you identify as the rock in your circle, grab a sheet of paper and write down the answers to the following questions:

What small task could you ask someone to do for you or
    help you with?
Who would you ask to help with this task?
How will you ask them? Phone, text, in person?
What will you say?

Got it all written down? Now go and ask them and then record your responses to the questions below:

How did they respond? Was it different from what you
    thought it would be?
If you ask for help again, will you do it the same way or try
    another approach? How did it feel to ask for help?

Now that we've discussed some of the personal attributes necessary to hold space for others, let's talk about what this actually looks like in practice. The three skills needed to hold space for someone are active listening, freedom from distraction, and a spirit of curiosity. These are all skills that we're taught as therapists in training to create spaces for clients to share, but they're great to use in our one-on-one friendships and sister circles as well.

Active Listening

The most powerful way to communicate that you are "there" with someone while they are sharing or going through something is to engage in active listening. Active listening involves listening intently while someone else shares, all with the expressed goal of hearing what they are saying. Oftentimes when others are speaking, we are not listening to hear, but instead we are listening to respond. This is actually a very easy pattern to fall into, especially with people we know well because we've spent so much time with them that we can anticipate a story and sometimes even finish their sentences. While this may suggest a particular type of intimacy, unfortunately it can also communicate impatience and a lack of interest in allowing them to share. A helpful strategy for ensuring that we are listening actively is through repeating and rephrasing what we've heard someone say. We are not making an interpretation about what they've said, but simply summarizing what we've heard them say and checking in for accuracy.

For example, let's say that one of your girlfriends calls you and is frustrated because she just found out her supervisor has convened several meetings with other members of her team that she was not included in when she is the one leading the project. She might say, "Girl, I am so done! Tell me why that sorry excuse for a supervisor has been meeting with several members of my team about the project I am leading and has not invited me to a meeting! What does that look like to the rest of the team if the leader of the project is not present? I knew I should have left this job when I had the chance." Here's how you could respond: "Girl, what? So you're telling me that your supervisor has been attempting to undermine you by talking to your co-workers without your knowledge? Is that right?" This response reflects that you've heard what she shared and can tell it back to her using your own words. This example also illustrates tone-matching, another important part of active listening. The words the friend uses in this example indicate that she's pretty annoyed and activated. When you respond in a way that matches her tone, it further communicates that you really hear and feel what she's saying. Consider for a minute that you are the friend who has been undermined by her supervisor and you share this experience with another sister. How would you feel if your friend's response is "Aw, man, that's messed up"? It doesn't quite match the intensity of what you've shared, does it? Do you feel like you want to open up and share more about what's happening? Probably not. Matching the tone of your sister both validates what she is feeling and signals that it is okay to continue.

Something to be aware of when we're holding space is that we should be doing more listening than talking when we're engaging in active listening. When loved ones share something painful, or if we feel they may be experiencing some shame in the conversation, sometimes we will recount a similar story to the one they've shared as a way of letting them know they're not alone. And while our intentions may be good in wanting to connect with them in this way, the unintentional impact could be to center our story in the space instead of theirs.

Freedom from Distraction

I know that I am not the only one trying to listen to the newest episode of my favorite podcast while simultaneously getting the kids ready for bed and figuring out my schedule for the next day. Many of us are in a constant loop of going and doing. Sometimes the only time I have to talk to my friends is on the commute to and from the kids' baseball practice. While this may be efficient, it isn't always very impactful. Sure, it may be a good way to catch up on mundane, day-to-day stuff, but in those situations where a sister really needs us to hold space for her, a quick chat before your next Zoom call is probably not going to cut it. It isn't always possible, but when it is, clearing a space for your sister to share with you without the distractions of kids, phones, or your never-ending to-do list is ideal. When someone needs to share something difficult with us, it can be hard to do so if they know that we're counting down the minutes until the next thing we need to rush off to.

To my earlier point, this is why it's important to know yourself well enough to recognize when you have the capacity to hold space for someone. It is 100 percent okay to offer another time that may work better for you if you know that the time she wants to talk won't work. It is better to offer up a time when you can actually commit to being with her fully than to agree to the conversation when you know you're distracted and maybe annoyed at having to squeeze one more thing into an already packed day. The bottom line is, offer what you can give as opposed to focusing on what you can't. It's okay to say, "I love you, girl, and I want to be there as much as I can, but right now I have X, Y, and Z going on. Can I do this for you?" I think it's also important to note that we may find ourselves in situations with sisters where they are asking for more than we can give at the moment. It's okay to be honest about this and to reinforce this boundary by setting your notifications to Do Not Disturb or by waiting until you do have more bandwidth to respond to a message.

A Spirit of Curiosity

Creating a space for our sisterfriends that is nonjudgmental is not always an easy feat. Sometimes in our attempts to learn more about what someone is sharing, we ask questions that come across more as accusations than invitations to expand. One way to avoid falling into this trap is to approach these conversations with a spirit of curiosity, an honest interest in diving deeper into what has happened and how she might feel about it. When we are curious about something, we aren't typically judging it. We want to know more about it. This helps us engage empathically. In our conversations with our sisterfriends, curiosity allows us to get the fullest picture of the story. The best way to demonstrate curiosity is to start off with an inquiry: "Tell me more about . . ." Let's return to the example of the friend whose supervisor is being shady. In this case, you could say something like "Tell me more about how you felt when you found out about these meetings" or "Tell me more about your relationship with your supervisor. Is this the first time they've done something like this?" These questions open up the option for her to share more and allow you to get a fuller idea of why she may be experiencing this situation the way she is.

Whether it's one-on-one with our bestie from way back, in our girlfriend sister circles, or even among women we don't intimately know, vulnerability and care have the capacity to usher in healing.

This is why learning how to hold space and how to be held are invaluable skills to possess. I know it's not easy. Even when we say we want spaces for intimacy and vulnerability, we don't always know how to get there, and sometimes it doesn't feel comfortable. But my hope is that I've been able to offer you a little bit of guidance on the road to getting better at it. Because that's why we're here, right? To get a little better at creating and flourishing in these sacred sisterhood spaces.

QUESTIONS FOR REFLECTION

1. What have you been taught about vulnerability? Do you find that it is easier for you to be vulnerable with certain people or in certain situations? What commonalities exist?

2. When was the last time space was held for you? What felt most impactful about it?

3. When someone is listening to you, what kinds of things let you know they really hear you? When you are listening to others, what kinds of things do you do to demonstrate that you're listening?

CHAPTER 5

There Is Space for Everyone in the Circle

What if the mightiest word is love? /
love with no need to pre-empt grievance.

–*Elizabeth Alexander*

Journalist Elisha Beach writes, "Friendship with other Black women offers a safe space. We can be things Black women aren't expected to be . . . silly, soft, sensitive, vulnerable. We aren't concerned we will get pigeonholed into being the 'strong Black woman' or the 'angry Black woman.' We know our [sisters] see us as the multifaceted people we can be."[1] This is absolutely right. There is no one else who knows the particular weight of our armor, the ways we've been required to be strong, mostly for others, than another Black woman. Nowhere does this feel truer than when there is yet another instance of a gross and tragic injustice perpetrated against our community. I find that in those times, one of the most powerful ways to help regulate my feelings is being in community with my sisterfriends.

WHEN WILL IT STOP?

I'd been struggling after this last mass shooting. I find myself searching for the exits when I go to the grocery or to the movies. I get startled when a car backfires on the street. My daughter knows more about how to respond in an active-shooter situation than she ever should. When will it stop? Fear and rage and sadness filled my whole body up and sometimes it felt like I couldn't see straight. Some friends of mine came to visit me for a couple of days and while we were supposed to be working on our creative projects together, there were moments when they could just look at me and tell that I wasn't present. It wasn't some overt, therapy-like thing either. They weren't digging for information. They would just stop and say, "You alright? You want to go take a walk? You want to go ride our bikes?" I felt seen. With each acknowledgment, it felt like a valve had been released.

—Nisha, 47

I'd found myself in a similar space following the horrible mass shooting that occurred in Buffalo, New York, on May 14, 2022. Ten Black people, many of them elders in the community, were murdered. So many women I spoke with found themselves reeling with sorrow and grief at this news. It felt like there were no breaks, no time to sit and process what had happened. We just had to jump back on our Zoom calls the next day at work, smiling and pretending to be present. And, yes, maybe that's an extreme example, but I'm not sure it's really that much different for Black women in more commonplace scenarios. Just going into the office and dealing with everyday microaggressions frequently requires us to put on our armor in order to create a kind of distance needed to get through the day. So for those who have actually lived with being directly impacted by racial violence, events like the Buffalo shooting or the latest images of Black people being beaten or killed by police officers can be triggering. We are forced to relive our own personal trauma while still trying to navigate the world. It often feels like there are no days off; frankly, it is exhausting.

I have found, and many sisters concur, that in these instances vulnerability within sisterhood and having a sacred space to share are healing and life-giving. In fact, that is exactly what we did as a community on the Thursday following the Buffalo massacre. We used our Three for Thursday time to check in with one another, cry, and validate the rage, sadness, and fear that many of us were feeling.

It's important to note that the goal of holding space isn't always to come up with a solution to a problem. Sometimes it's more about being seen, heard, and affirmed. There is nothing any of us could have said to one another that would have made things better. However, simply being available to help a sister we know carry the weight of her sorrow, even if it's shared sorrow, can be powerful. While this was not a situation that required problem-solving, I must note that even in situations where it may be easier to problem-solve, doing so may not always be what is needed. Create a space where your sister feels sufficiently heard, then ask, "Do you want to do some problem-solving together, or do you simply want me to sit with you in this situation?" This exchange will allow her to tell you what she needs. Typically, our intentions to jump into problem-solving mode are pure because we don't like to see someone we care about hurting or frustrated, but if we offer solutions too fast, we can inadvertently send a message that her feelings are a burden. We also run the risk of truncating her experience of fully processing her feelings about what's happened in the interest of finding a quick fix.

In chapter 4, we talked a lot about what's needed to hold space for our sisters in the one-on-one dynamic. Your girlfriend from college. Your close sisterfriend at the job. However, in a circle of sisters the factor that is most important in being able to create a space where everyone knows they can be held is for each individual within the group to know what role they play in maintaining the circle. If we refer back to the Three for Thursday example I shared earlier, some sisters were more vocal in sharing their feelings about what happened in Buffalo, others silently cried, a few shared books and other resources to help process grief, and still others shared avenues of support for the families in Buffalo. If you think about it, I am sure your sister circles function in a similar way. Everyone does something different with the same intention of loving on the person or people in need. There is absolutely space for the different ways in which each of us shows up in our circles.

Think about the last gathering you had with a group of your sisterfriends. Who organized it? Who was the first to arrive? Who was the last to leave? Who was supposed to show up but never did? My guess is that it was probably fairly easy for you to come up with an answer to each of these questions without much thought because there is a good chance that the sister who organized your last gathering is the one who organizes most of them and the sister who didn't show up may have a habit of missing events. Whether we are conscious of it or not, we tend to take on roles within groups that aid in the cohesiveness and continuance of the group. I love what psychologist Thema Bryant writes about this: "For social support to be effective it needs to be mutually beneficial, grounded in common values/priorities, based in authenticity, accepting, truth-telling, and growth promoting. The social support literature describes both emotional support and instrumental support. There are sister friends who give comfort and then there are those who give resources. At times you may find sister friends who give both."[2] What she seems to suggest is that while both emotional and instrumental support are needed and should be present in the sister circle as a whole, not every individual sister is going to offer both. It's highly likely that each sister will have a role she tends to play that contributes to the cohesiveness of the group.

In my experience working with Black women in groups, sisters tend to fall into one of four roles: the Leader, the Wallflower, the Firecracker, and the Peacemaker. These roles are not at all static or absolute. We actually may find ourselves moving in and out of different roles depending on the setting or situation, but they do give us some information about how we show up in communal spaces. Here's a little more about each role:

The Leader—The leader is the one who offers organization to the group. She is typically the one making sure y'all are getting together regularly, and she's probably the one you thought about when I asked who organized the last get-together. She is also the one who often feels the most responsible for the emotional wellness of the group. It's not uncommon for her to be the one checking in with others about how they're feeling and making sure that the group stays tight-knit. In many cases, she is the strong friend. While her attention to detail and organizational skills keep her very involved with the group, it's also very easy for her to be somewhat invisible because she spends a lot of time tending to others and is seen as capable. Unfortunately, it isn't always apparent that she needs to be checked on as well. You may recognize her from our discussion about the paradox of the rock in chapter 4.

The Wallflower—The wallflower is the sister within the group who generally sits quietly and listens as others talk. However, when she does speak, it's super impactful. She is often paying more attention to what's not being said than what is. She's very loyal to the group and won't typically miss any gatherings, but she's not at all likely to be the one planning them. If there is a conflict in the group, she'd prefer to be left out of it. When you think about the phrase "still waters run deep," you'd be thinking of her.

The Firecracker—The firecracker is the sister who will say the thing that needs to be said, but not always gently. Along with the leader, the firecracker tends to take up most of the space in the group. She's likely the life of the party, but if the party goes off the rails, she's probably the one involved in that too. The group typically values her insights because she says the things that others won't. When you need someone to hype you up or give you the courage to do the hard thing, the firecracker is the one to call. She will ride shotgun when you need to defend yourself.

The Peacemaker—The peacemaker is the sister who will send the "We need to talk" text message. If two other sisters in the group are having a conflict, she's likely to call each of them individually and then encourage them to hash out their issues. She is also likely to struggle with setting boundaries in the group and can easily fall into a pattern of pleasing people. She tends to be very reliable and the one you want to call when you need someone to affirm you after a tough day.

Paying attention to the roles we play in a group not only provides insight into our strengths and where we naturally shine, but also sheds light on the areas that may be difficult for us and require some work. For example, if we look at the leader's tendency to get so caught up in taking care of others that she is not getting her own needs met, what kind of impact might we see? We'd likely see resentment at some point and a sense of feeling undervalued that may result in her no longer wanting to be a part of the group. And what about the peacemaker? Her tendency to people-please may eventually make it difficult for her to stand up for herself in the group, thereby lessening the closeness she feels to the other members. As the proverb says, "Wherever we go, there we are." The roles that we assume in the group with our sisterfriends can provide us with valuable information about how we relate to others; more important, the group affords us an opportunity to examine our relationship to these roles to determine if it's one we'd like to continue.

To be absolutely clear, these roles are not like parts you would play on a stage. You're not bound to them. It's not mandatory that the peacemaker shows up that way in every single scenario or circumstance. These roles are really just designed for you to get information for yourself about your tendencies as they relate to your sister circle. I don't want sisters closing this book and thinking, *Well, I'm the peacemaker. I'm going to be that—all day, every day.* You will burn out that way, for sure. It is always okay for the person who tends to be the caretaker of the group to say, "Hey, I feel like I'm the only one who cares when there's tension in the group. Can we agree as a circle to do something differently so that I'm not the one who always has to pull us together?" It's also possible for members of the group to share roles or to call out someone who has taken their role too far. If the firecracker's "truth-telling" deeply offends people, then it's okay to tell her, "Ouch! That hurt!" and open up a conversation on when enough is enough. Again, I created these roles not to throw another label at us but to offer a starting place for reflection. They simply provide data for understanding how we are showing up.

When I think about holding space in our sister circles, there is no clearer example than a scene from the final season of one of my favorite television shows, *Girlfriends*. We can get into a discussion later about the lack of closure many of us feel because we were robbed of a proper goodbye to the show, but for now, let's look at what was happening in that final season, which included only Joan, Maya, and Lynn as the main characters (Toni, the fourth girlfriend, had exited). It begins with Joan finally getting what appears to be the happily ever after she has always wanted. She is engaged to Aaron, and they've just purchased a new home together. As they are settling in, Aaron finds out that he is being deployed to Iraq. In episode 2 of the season, Joan, who is the poster child for the leader role, drops him off at the airport and comes home only to collapse into a puddle of tears in her kitchen.

The next morning, when her girls come to check on her, she thanks them for dropping by but tells them they shouldn't have. While they are attempting to hold space and allow her to share how she's feeling, she says she wants to talk about something lighter and opens the oven to a pan full of Lynn's favorite cupcakes to celebrate her finally getting a talent manager. In subsequent episodes, we see Joan dealing with Aaron's deployment by prepping care packages to send to Iraq. Lynn is beginning to blossom in her singing career. Maya is trying to write her third book and has also recently found out that she is expecting a new baby.

In episode 4 of the season, we learn that Maya has had a miscarriage and, of course, her girls rally around to offer her support. She too insists that she is fine. Joan, being who she is, attempts to open space for Maya to be honest and confront her feelings about the miscarriage by taking her shopping. While at the store, Maya discovers that Joan is carrying around a purse full of clippings about the war in Iraq and now realizes that Joan is not handling Aaron's deployment as well as they all might have thought. She calls Lynn down to the store to stage an intervention, and when they begin to question Joan about why she's carrying around the newspaper clippings she lashes out and accuses them of not caring to ask about Aaron since the day after he'd left. She shares that she was tired of always being the one checking on everyone else while no one ever checks on her. Lynn says that she hasn't checked in because she doesn't want to remind Joan that he is gone. Maya responds by saying she just doesn't have the words—doesn't know what to say—to which Joan replies, "Say anything!"

This is such a great illustration of several things we've discussed so far. We see the role that each of them plays in the group—Joan as a leader, Lynn as a wallflower, and Maya as a firecracker/peacemaker. We also see how the roles Joan and Maya play impact not only their abilities to hold space for the other sisters in their circle but also their own ability to be held. There is no clearer example of the paradox of the rock than Joan experiencing a breakdown in the dressing room on a shopping trip she planned to make Maya feel better. And finally, we see what it may look like when we are not intentional about holding space when it's needed or asking for it. What may have been different if Joan had shared how sad she was the day after Aaron left instead of minimizing it? How could Lynn and Maya have pushed past their own discomfort about how Joan *might* feel to explore how she actually felt? Who in our lives reminds us of any of the characters from this example? Who are we in the example?

Of course, it can be fun to dissect the behaviors of fictional characters and take what morsels have meaning for our own lives, but it's likely even more impactful to look at your own circle to consider how well you all are doing at holding space for one another and what might need some work. Here are a few questions to help you gauge where you stand:

1. Do you think that everyone in your circle feels welcome to share when they're struggling with something?

2. How does your role in your sister circle impact how you hold space for others? How do you think it impacts others' ability to hold space for you?

3. Is there an "elephant in the room" in your sister circle that the group has been avoiding? What do you think is making it difficult to address?

Sometimes the roles we play have everything to do with the homeostasis of the circle. Because if somebody already tends to be the firecracker in the group, does the group need another one? That might be one too many sparks, Sis. Maybe you need to lean into a different role at times so that the group feels balanced and cohesive? Again, these roles are not static in any way, but understanding them does help with group cohesiveness and a sense of belonging. And it's true that different groups will call out different pieces of you. Who you once were with your college girlfriends— maybe the peacemaker—makes it easy to fall back into that role even if in other areas of your life you have matured or turned into somebody different, say, the leader. In any case, let's take a look at how we can be most effective in whatever role we play within the group.

Every role within the group has the ability to help the healing process. For instance, the leader will be the one to organize whatever efforts are needed for support. If she sees something going wrong, she will likely jump into problem-solving mode. She is also likely to be at the forefront of any formal intervention that would happen for a member of the group. It will be incredibly important for the leader to remember to slow down occasionally and truly assess what the sister needs. Because leaders are natural problem solvers, they might not consider that the person seeking help actually just needs someone to sit and cry with them. Slowing down the process and asking the person directly what they need in the moment is a great skill for leaders to implement. Also, their problem-solving ability may be better served by the leader exercising some forethought. For example, sometimes when people are struggling they can't think about what they need. So asking if the person needs groceries delivered, or someone to watch the kids or to come over and do the dishes would be helpful.

Wallflowers might want to step out of their comfort zone and show up in a way that is different from their usual approach. Because wallflowers can be misinterpreted as being aloof or as not caring about what's going on, they will need to work very hard at letting the person know that they care and figuring out ways to be intentional within their own capacities.

Now, if I'm honest, my inclination is to say that the firecracker, first and foremost, needs to simply watch her mouth. But let me reframe that. In a scenario where a person needs support from the group, the firecracker might consider toning down her "voice" just a little. Especially when the pain is fresh for someone. Yes, sometimes a person needs to hear the hard truth, and generally there comes a time when the firecracker's truth-telling is needed. But timing matters. When a person is in the thick of it and needs to be held, a firecracker firing off hard truths can shift the attention from the person who requires the healing space to the firecracker. It's important that in all our truth-telling we aren't making the situation about us.

And finally, peacemakers tend to shine in situations where space needs to be held for their sisters. They naturally do this well. I would just suggest that peacemakers be very careful that in an effort to keep the peace, they aren't being enablers or resisting holding a person accountable. Taking ownership of our portion of the challenge is part of the healing journey, and peacemakers who lack self-awareness might get in the way of that. Also, peacemakers should make sure they are actually allowing the person who needs space held for them to go through the natural course of grief. Try not to tamp down a sister's feelings or say things like "Please don't cry" or "It's going to be okay." Sometimes we need to scream or cry. Sometimes two sisters need to have it out. Sometimes we need to sit in discomfort to get to the other side of the pain. Sometimes there is no peace in the moment and that's got to be okay.

An African proverb says, "Women give birth with other women." I would add that "women give birth *to* other women." So much of our becoming is tied to our relationships with one another and how we hold our sisters down or not. Our ability to hold space for one another as Black women matters. No, we are not all the same. But we are the only ones who know what the particular kind of pain we experience in this world feels like. We have, in a way, been stranded in a world built on racist and oppressive systems. When we are able to sit with our sisters through the good, the bad, and the ugly, we become one another's lighthouses in a world that doesn't want us to have joy and peace and love. Being able to have spaces that we can go to where people don't think we're overreacting, where people really *see* us, is priceless. In the desert of white supremacy and patriarchy, we provide an oasis for one another. A place of nourishment, as bell hooks wrote in *Sisters of the Yam,* before we have to cross those sands again.

QUESTIONS FOR REFLECTION

1. Do the sisters in your circle fall into one of the roles described here? Who plays what role? Do you think they would agree with the role you've chosen for them?

2. Which role do you play in your sister circles? Is it consistent across spaces or does it change? If so, to what do you attribute the change?

3. At your next sister circle gathering, have a discussion about the role each of you plays in your circle. Create a space for everyone to share what they enjoy about their role and how they'd like some additional support.

CHAPTER 6

Sisters over Systems

Sisters are more than the sum of their relative
disadvantages: they are active agents who
craft meaning out of their circumstances and do so
in complicated and diverse ways.

–*Melissa Harris-Perry*

Systems that were instrumental in building the foundation of
our country—patriarchy, white supremacy, colorism, ageism,
misogynoir—were never meant to truly serve Black women. Not
only do these systems impact us as individuals, but they also impact the quality of our relationships with one another overall.
How we show up in our personal sister circles has a deep impact
on how we show up for the sisters we don't know or don't call
"friend" as well as for Black women globally who are confronted
with systems and systemic challenges that try to tear us down and
apart. We've already discussed how our personal sister circles sit
inside the larger global circle of sisters, so it makes sense that how
we navigate these circles, big and small, is inevitably impacted by
the systems that govern them in our society.

WHO DO YOU THINK YOU ARE?

I've had amazing relationships with the women in my life.
I'm still very close to friends I've had since high school and
college. But one of my biggest challenges has been feeling
the "sisterhood" from women I work with. In fact, working as

a professor in academia, I've found it so hard to build meaningful relationships with fellow Black women. I recently have been called upon by my college to lead much of our diversity, equity, and inclusion efforts, especially around our hiring practices. This required me to gain buy-in from the department heads. Now, there are very few Black women who head departments on our campus anyway, but one woman, a full professor with over thirty years of teaching under her belt, has made my work life a living hell. She actually said to me, "Who are you to get all of this praise for work I've been trying to do for twenty-five or thirty years? How dare you not follow these rules?" I was never trying to step on this sister's toes but she didn't see it that way. Honestly, I feel so alone in this work and could have used some of her guidance.

—Marsha, 35

Ouch! This one stings. It would be relatively easy to write off this woman's response to Marsha as an "all skinfolk ain't kinfolk" situation, but I think it's important for us to unpack and peel back the layers to consider how, particularly in work environments, varying value systems and generational differences can impact how we see our sisters. From 2016 to 2019, I was the director of the Counseling Center at Clark Atlanta University. My administrative assistant was Ms. Joyce Worrell, a woman many years my senior. No matter how many times Ms. Joyce told me I didn't have to, I couldn't call her solely by her first name. I come from a time and family where it's required to "put a handle" on the names of elders: Ms. Martha, Sis Terry, Cousin Laura. If they are older than me by more than a decade, they are addressed accordingly. And despite being her supervisor and being in an academic setting, I felt the same way about Ms. Joyce. It felt weird to call her anything else. It sometimes felt weird to tell her what to do period.

Ms. Joyce had been at CAU forever. She knew the ins and outs of the role I was in, and while I'd heard horror stories from my peers who were also navigating situations where the generational gap caused conflict, thankfully, Ms. Joyce was incredibly support-ive of me and wanted me to be successful. Yes, she could have set me up to fail because she didn't want to work with somebody so young, but she didn't. She walked me through the position and gave me a heads-up on all the potential land mines. She truly ushered me through the role as opposed to resenting me for it.

Our relationship turned out great, but I think it's important to consider the factors that could have influenced it negatively, some of which may have been at play with Marsha's colleague in deter-mining how Marsha's colleague interacted with her. First and fore-most, the systems of white supremacy that are deeply rooted in every major institution thrive on creating competition between and among Black folks, and Black women in particular, with the prize being some mirage of safety that comes with proximity to whiteness. White supremacy says that if we *must* have a Black person, there can only be one. There's never going to be a scenario where everybody's winning. So in order to get to the top of what-ever ladder they're climbing, some people are going to step on folks who look like them to get there.

While it may be easy to blame the sisters who take this path, it's imperative that we shift our focus to examining and dismantling the systems that create an environment where some Black women have become socialized to fight one another for some coveted spot at the top of a crumbling capitalistic food chain. The truth is that most of us are just trying to do the best we can to survive. How-ever, what if we understood and acted from a place of unity? Could we do more than survive if we decided to hold space for our sisters even if it's inconvenient? If we join forces, we might be able to change the systems that are trying to bind us. If we refuse to play the games "they" have set up, we can be strategic in build-ing our own systems while dismantling theirs. In that way, our sisterhood becomes a form of resistance.

HOLDING THE DOOR OPEN
BEHIND YOU VS. CLOSING IT SHUT

I believe that the primary way to gauge our role in either perpetu-
ating systems of oppression or dismantling them can be found in
whether we would describe ourselves (or perhaps more accurately,
whether others would describe us) as a sister who holds the door
open for others when she enters a space or a sister who promptly
closes it behind her. Stay with me now—sisterhood calls for honest and sometimes difficult conversations. As sad as it is, we are
well into the twenty-first century and still finding ourselves with
firsts: The first Black woman on the Supreme Court. The first
Black woman to win *Big Brother*. The first Black woman puppe-
teer on *Sesame Street*. This is where we are, so it is not uncommon
for us to find ourselves as "the only one" in any given situation.
The real question is, what do we do when we find ourselves there,
and how does this impact sisters in our surroundings? Some of us
find ourselves in this position and immediately start the work of
figuring out how to fill the space with others who look like us
(holding the door open). Others of us relish our roles, feeling that
somehow we've made it solely because we had just the right com-
bination of luck, hard work, and networking. It has likely been
treacherous to get where we are and so we go about protecting this
"coveted" spot as if our life depended on it. We actively work to
hoard resources and are often adversarial with other sisters (closing the door shut).

Take a minute to think about your last experience with another
Black woman in a more senior role than you. Was she the only
Black woman in that leadership position? What kind of assessments did you and other sisters do to figure out whether she was
on your side or not? Come on, don't act like many Black women
don't have a process we use to vet a sister if we're not sure about
her. Granted, some sisters come into a space and their reputation
for not being on the "home team" precedes them, so no assessment is necessary, but for the others, there is a clear probationary
period.

Any Black woman who values community and connection understands that there is a way to enter a space when working with other sisters to let them know they're safe with you. It probably goes something like this: At first you are cordial to the other Black women, but not too friendly just yet because you can't make the non-Black folks in the office too suspicious. This progresses to perhaps brief lunch meetings where the other sisters share some background and give you more of the lay of the land. It eventually concludes with a brunch or dinner, off-site and probably far away from the office, where you're able to be real and allow them to see more of who you are, establishing a sense of safety.

Given these descriptions, I think we can fairly assume that Marsha's colleague is someone who has likely decided to close the door behind her. It's very likely that she cut her teeth at the college when there was no possible way for diversity roundtables and professional programs on race and gender to have been well received. Maybe many of the changes she longed to make, that she tried to make, had been rejected time and time again. What would it have been like for this elder to instead say how proud she was of Marsha and ask how she could assist her now that the administration seemed more open to new ideas? What would it have been like for her to share with her younger colleague some of the plans she'd been trying to move forward in the hope that Marsha would be able to assist her in gaining some traction? Yes, we can challenge her bad behavior against her colleague, but we also must point several fingers at the system that fostered and encouraged that resentment to grow in the first place.

I do believe that we can't have a discussion about white supremacy in Marsha's story without talking about how ageism shows up. For Black women, generational differences and challenges seem to come up most in the workplace. The way that younger sisters are showing up in these spaces—more liberated, more empowered—feels radically different from how it was in years past. The recent passing of the CROWN Act in several states means that Black women can wear their hair in locs or braids or cornrows without legally sanctioned repercussion from their employer. Movements like #MeToo and #ChurchToo mean that women are being more vocal about the ways in which we've been harmed in professional and organizational spaces. Again, this allows younger women to show up free in ways that older women were not able to and are not accustomed to.

While not a threat to our sisterhood specifically, ageism can create conflicts that make it challenging to engage one another in these settings. There is a difference between when an elder says, "Oh you can't do that. We've never done that before" as opposed to "Go off, Li'l Sis!" That feeling is different. It's an empowerment that can be so fulfilling, and I want us to tap into it more. Younger sisters can recognize the work and challenges their elders endured to get us to this point, and older sisters can cheer on the youngins who are taking the baton and running like Flo-Jo with it.

And I know that many Gen X or earlier folks might be thinking, *But Dr. Joy, they are taking things too far.* I hear that. As I've shared, there are some demonstrations of vulnerability, especially on the internet and social media, that may seem over the top or rooted in naïveté. I've watched posts on social media myself and thought, *Baby, just keep living*—the Black elder's variation of "Get off my lawn!" But maybe it's important for those of us who are older to interrogate why these displays of vulnerability, of putting it all out there, make us uncomfortable. If this is the case for you, what comes up when you see a younger sister share in this way? Is your sense of protection activated? Is there some part of you that longs for this behavior in your own life? Or is it something else? Yes, it could be that we are wise enough to know that no one in their twenties has fully realized the consequences of their actions. But it could also be that their freedom rubs up against our chains. So there is harmony and balance available to us here.

We can respect the wisdom of older generations and celebrate the liberation of the younger ones. It would serve Gen X and earlier to foster genuine relationships with millennials and Gen Zers so we can recognize the love we have for and need from one another. Offering any kind of feedback in the confines of a relationship as opposed to random commentary online or in our siloed groups will matter more to our global sisterhood than anything. Culturally, intergenerational relationships have always been valuable to and for Black women. It is how traditions and stories have been passed on, and in many cases, it has ensured our survival.

THE FRUITS OF A ROTTEN TREE

Working closely with Black women in individual and group therapy settings, I have seen the tensions that can surface when we are not aware of our tender spots and their origins: the quickness with which we put up walls, the speed with which we disengage, and the hurt that bubbles up from feeling ignored or unheard. When I see friction between sisters, whether in real time or on a reality television show, I have to ask, "What's going on that's causing these reactions?" There is often a root cause to be uncovered. I don't believe that Black women are simply "mean girls" or have bad attitudes. The root is typically a by-product of one of the faulty systems I discussed earlier. Learning to recognize the triggers that result from these systemic challenges and examining the true "why" can help us as a community to strengthen our bonds.

White supremacy has birthed myriad systemic barriers that impact Black women in the areas of economics (homeownership and building wealth), our working lives (work advancement and Black women's pay gap), our familial relations (sibling rivalry and family strife), and dating (colorism and hair texture). These barriers often lead to increased stress and strain for Black women and a tendency to operate in survival mode as the odds are often stacked against us.

Operating in survival mode typically means that we are not grounded, not thinking rationally, and not able to embrace a spirit of abundance because abundance is not a priority when survival is threatened. Think about it like this: When we are in real danger—let's say a bear is chasing us—our body does what it is designed to do. It goes into survival mode to give us the best chance at making it out of this situation alive. Adrenaline starts pumping to our brain and parts of our body to allow us to mobilize. Our heart rate increases. Our lungs expand to enable us to take in as much oxygen as possible, and this plentiful supply of oxygen makes us more alert and heightens all of our senses because these are the things we will need to survive this chase. When the danger has passed, the bear is gone, our brain sends out the "all clear" signal that allows our heart rate to decrease and our breathing to return to normal; the systems in our body that were highly engaged can now go back to normal functioning. But what happens when we are in a constant state of running from the bear (i.e., constantly confronted with systemic barriers)? The chronic activation of our stress response can lead to things like high blood pressure, heart disease, and psychological distress.

So what then is there to do with all of this? How do our relationships with one another thrive when there are so many systems invested in our discord and disease? Much of this "crabs in the barrel" dynamic, as it's referenced in the culture, comes from the way enslaved Africans were pitted against one another during the transatlantic slave trade. It's where colorism was birthed and allowed to thrive. Because of Eurocentric beauty standards that evolved from white supremacy, lighter-skinned Black people were treated differently from darker-skinned Black people. And I use "differently" intentionally because to assume "better" in the context of slavery ignores rape and sexual assault and the other horrors that came with being perceived as more beautiful. The bar is quite literally in hell. So clearly the residue of all this still exists today. All skinfolk ain't kinfolk and, yes, there are some Black women, impacted or influenced by the system of white supremacy, who might choose to cordon off or compartmentalize themselves, their Blackness, in order to achieve whatever definition of success they've chosen to embrace. These might also be the sisters we leave behind. For the moment.

Leave a sister behind, Dr. Joy? Say it isn't so.

I know. I know. That doesn't sound very therapist of me, but I'm a firm believer that there comes a time when we must love people from a distance. Some of our greatest healing work as individuals and as a collective will come from being okay with this. This is not to say that we wish any ill will on women who are entangled with white supremacy to the extent that they would turn on their sisters. We can even still love them and long for the day when they return to the fold. But if it's clear that a sister doesn't value the very concept of a global sisterhood, if it's not a core value for her, then we simply aren't going in the same direction.

Sisterhood is a given for Black women, based on our history and culture. But you have to opt in. By virtue of being Black women, we are born into this experience. But our free will and the pressure of these crooked systems mean that it's not necessarily something that every Black woman values. If proximity to whiteness and all that one might believe comes with that is of greater importance, then we can't necessarily play in the same sandbox. There's a quote that's often falsely attributed to Harriet Tubman that says, "I freed a thousand slaves. I could have freed a thousand more if only they knew they were slaves." I'd like to think that what Mother Harriet actually said was "I'm freeing some folks. You can come with me. But if you are fighting me to stay on this plantation, then I'm certainly not fighting to take you from it."

If, for whatever reason, you find yourself valuing yourself in relation to your proximity to whiteness, then it might be time to take a minute to reflect and evaluate what you're doing and why you're doing it. Listen, I don't think many of us get to where we are without having to play the game. But the trick is that you have to actually recognize it as a game. You have to remind yourself, "Yes, there are some things I need to do to get ahead and feed my family, but getting ahead for getting ahead's sake is really not one of my values. My values are sisterhood. My values are leaving the door open for as many people as possible." Affirming *that* is how you don't get sucked into the system. And if you do get sucked in, once you realize it—or another sister brings it to your attention— you immediately work toward recommitting yourself to the core values you say you have. And maybe that means more mentoring or the utilization of other resources to ensure that you do not "backslide" on your sisters again.

Championing sisterhood and helping us heal from what these systems have wrought in our bodies and minds is liberation work. So anyone, including another sister, who disrupts our liberation, or our freedom—for whatever reason, fear, discomfort, uncertainty, whatever—can stay exactly where she is. Until she's ready to do that recommittal. When and if Sis is able to understand and correctly identify the true enemy that divides us, then we all can course-correct to experience the fullness of the collective and continue on our healing journey.

Now listen, I don't want to oversimplify the toll these systems can have on our lives and the ease with which one can disentangle from their grips. Again, we all do what we feel we must to survive, but if you find yourself as a Black woman seeing success through the narrow and warped view that is set up via white supremacy, I do invite you to consider the stability and impact of that success. Is it long-lasting, and what did/do you have to sacrifice to maintain it? What do your connections and support look like? If it were gone tomorrow, what would you be left with? How comfortable is it to be who you are in the space? Your answers to these questions can help to clarify your values and provide insight into how to change course if that's something you desire.

Beyond leaving sisters who don't value our sisterhood behind, how we choose to navigate white supremacist systems can cause us to make small compromises that impact our sisterfriendships. For example, if you get a promotion or an opportunity at work, but by accepting that opportunity you may put your sisterfriend colleague in a bind, what do you do? There's a system at work here that could create a divide between the two of you. You want and need to take the opportunity because it advances your career, but you don't want to hurt your friend. (By the way, even the idea that we have to question our ability to take the opportunity, not because of how it will impact Suzy and Chad, but because it will directly impact Tasha, is problematic.) If you are in community with the sister, then a conversation needs to happen. Can you go to your sisterfriend in the workplace and say, "This is hard for me, I'm wrestling with this, but I feel like I got to do this and I'm aware that it might leave you in a terrible spot. Can we put together a plan for how to make this less of a blow to you?"

Open communication will always be the next step toward managing the damage that can come to our relationships from external sources. When the fruit of white supremacy or patriarchy weighs us down, we have to touch back to the community that got us wherever we are, or the sister who was there with you along the way. Let's remain in constant communication with our sisters when there's the potential for conflict. If you see it on the horizon, don't run away from it. Don't ignore it and hope she doesn't notice. Have the conversation that says, "Okay, they're going to try to pit us against each other. How are we going to handle this? What's our game plan?" Maybe there's a way for both of you to get what you want. Or maybe this is a moment when one person gets theirs and comes back and scoops her sister when she has the power and resources to do so. Everyone knows what's going on. No one is blindsided. The relationship is saved.

It's also important to evaluate a sister's capacity, especially as you are making this plan. Is your work sister near burnout? Is she going to be able to follow through with the strategy, or because of simply being exhausted by the shenanigans, will she decide to cave to the system? White supremacy is often, if not always, driven by capitalism. So a conversation about the way white supremacy threatens sisterhood cannot be divorced from the way capitalism can shift how we engage with one another. Now that you've gotten your promotion, can your sisterfriends at work still speak to you? Or do you believe that your leveling up makes them out of your league? Despite the only difference between you before promotion and you after is the additional responsibilities on your desk and zeros in your check.

Ain't I a Woman?

Patriarchy is not that much different from white supremacy in the way it threatens our sisterhoods and pits us against one another and facilitates scarcity as lifestyle. Even if Black people are at the top of whatever ladder we're climbing, there might be room for only one woman. And if one of us gets up there, then there definitely can't be more than one. I'm not looking at this solely through the lens of how men treat us. Unfortunately, internalized misogyny is a thing. Some sisters have bought into the lies about what women should or should not do. If you are a sister who challenges those notions, who is trying to live a more liberated life outside of what society has deemed appropriate, then some sisters are going to have a problem with that. Some of our sisters become frustrated by others who don't "follow the rules" because it activates their own perceived limitations.

Take, for instance, how many Black women will side with misogynist men when they spout horrible views on what makes a good woman. So many of these men's platforms are lucrative only because Black women have bought into their lies. We have internalized the idea that there's something wrong with us as women and that's why we can't find a partner, why we aren't successful, why we aren't worthy, etc., when in actuality it is the environment created by patriarchy intersecting with white supremacy that is the source of many of our challenges. And, of course, tension is often created within the sisterhood between those of us who see the scam in it all and those who don't. One sister is saying, "Girl, what are you doing? Why are you watching these people?" Another is saying, "No, maybe if I did submit more, I'd have more, be more . . ." We then turn on one another while the system benefits.

Patriarchy also impacts our relationships with one another because we tend to view our sisters through the same lens under which we are scrutinized. In a patriarchal system, we are often deconstructed, criticized, and assessed to see how we measure up. Our worthiness is frequently quantified through things like education, financial status, attractiveness, etc. And, of course, these are often some of the same approaches we use with one another as a means of assessing the competition for partners, jobs, and opportunities. The sizing one another up that happens and the whispers of "Who she think she is?" are holdovers from the ways that we are judged and only further harm our solidarity and perpetuate a chronically broken system.

So how does a sister navigate a relationship with another sister who has internalized this misogynoir?

Very gingerly.

At this point we need to figure out what conversations we can have with a person and which ones we can't because we will be left feeling frustrated. There will absolutely be times when we realize that we might not be able to have a conversation with a sister: *I've tried to talk to my girl about this thing multiple times and it never goes anywhere. So I'm not even going to go to this place with her anymore.*

Too often the internalized misogyny we see in our sisters is the result of a culture that has taught us to falsely value heteronormative relationships as some kind of prize. Even within the context of LGBTQIA or non-cis relationships, we're often taught that romantic relationships have higher value than our platonic friendships.

Most of us cannot unravel ourselves from patriarchy overnight. Healing within this context might mean being patient and extending grace to one another. It may mean offering resources to expand a sister's thinking and challenging these thoughts when they arise.

As I noted earlier, most of us have been socialized to believe that romantic relationships are the single most important pursuit of our lives. Deep down some of us believe that friendships are simply placeholders until we can find a romantic partner, but in fact our friendships are often profoundly impactful and can last even longer than many romantic relationships. And I can hear some sisters protesting: *You mean to tell me I'm not supposed to put my boo first?*

I'm actually not saying that at all. I'm suggesting that there is no hierarchy. There's no better or worse. It's more about how you are spending your energy. Is it possible to spend time with your significant other and your friends? If someone is spending all their time with their friends and not their spouse, we clearly understand that to be problematic. But wouldn't the opposite also be true? If you engage only with your boo and not with your sister-friends, then parts of you are likely not being fed.

We've been taught that our partners come first when really there should be a more balanced approach to all of our intimate relationships. Now don't get stuck here. Stay with me. Of course, if there is an emergency, and your partner needs you, then you might break plans with your friends to tend to that need. Your sisterfriends might actually tell you to go ahead and handle your business. But it's important to be aware of patterns. Are you always canceling on your girls? If girls' night has been on the calendar for months but all of a sudden your partner needs you to come help them find their dress shirt there might be something else happening that speaks to how you were socialized to show up in your relationships. Some of this comes from being born into very religious households. Many church doctrines promote a hierarchy in our relationships that prioritizes romantic unions over friendships and women being solely in positions of servitude. But even beyond the church, some of that socialization of partners-before-friends can come from the relationship dynamics we saw growing up. If we witnessed our mothers having rich friendships alongside reciprocal romantic relationships, then we might not buy into this, but from my observations, that hasn't always been the case.

Our sisterfriends shouldn't have second-tier status in our relationships. Yes, there will be plenty of times when our priorities will be our immediate families. But our intimate friendships should not be de-emphasized because of that. White supremacy teaches us to have a hierarchy mindset. Culturally, ancestrally, we've always been about the village. That hierarchical view is actually a departure for us. Psychotherapist and author Esther Perel speaks to this a lot in her work: how love relationships have become the center of our world but that this is actually not sustainable. It's not sustainable for you to think that just one person—your romantic partner—is going to be able to meet all of your needs.

Let's return to a more indigenous way of relating, centering the idea that we develop ourselves and our children in communities, not as people separate from one another. This means being just as intentional in making and keeping plans with our sisters. It means diversifying how we spend our time so that we are part of many different systems, lessening the chance of any one in particular becoming strained.

Is this another form of respectability politics? A formula for saying there is a certain way of being as a Black woman in relationship with others that's right? Perhaps. At the end of the day, I still trace it back to the two-headed beast of white supremacy and patriarchy that gets its kicks from causing us to pick one another apart. No matter the decision—whether to wear bonnets in public or not, or to hang with our girls while partnered or not—when under the influence of these systems we are so focused on the male gaze overall and the white male gaze in particular that we believe there's only one way to show up as a Black woman, even when that is clearly not the case. Our standard for the way we move and live and be has to be something other than the standard that was given to us.

So much of my discussion of the systems that threaten our sisterhood is about making sure that we know the external factors that impact us so that we can be better sisters. Awareness of what influences how we deal with one another is one step toward healing.

Unfortunately, it doesn't look like white supremacy and patriarchy are going anywhere anytime soon, but we should want to avoid the trap of the oppressed taking on the traits of the oppressor. We do this by extending compassion to one another, embracing our humanity, and creating spaces where everyone's needs are met. The place where this compassion and resistance feels most needed is in our thinking and talking about colorism.

SHADES OF LOVE

Colorism can be incredibly difficult to even talk about with one another. Many of us get hung up on its definition and never address how destructive it is. As noted earlier in the chapter, colorism at its core references the way darker-skinned people have been treated and positioned unfairly in society compared with lighter-skinned people. The conversation often becomes tenuous because lighter-skinned sisters also experience very valid pain surrounding complexion. But those dialogues exist in a separate space; they're not part of the discussion about colorism, which specifically addresses the inequities experienced by darker-skinned people. When the concerns of lighter-skinned sisters are brought into the conversation on colorism, division inevitably rears its head in the sisterhood. Once again, we find ourselves pointing the finger at one another as opposed to the systems that have created this polarity.

How do we get to a place where we can have this conversation with our sisters and where everybody's pain can be held without taking away from what colorism actually is? In spaces where sisters gather regularly, opening up dialogue about how our lives and relationships with one another are impacted by colorism can be helpful. Guidelines for the conversation should be centered on a shared understanding of what colorism is. Because I know that this can quickly go off the rails, I'd like to offer you a few questions that may help to ground this topic:

1. How do you see colorism play out in your communities?

2. What do you wish more people understood about how colorism impacts our relationships with one another?

3. What do you think we can do as sisters to resist the impact that colorism has on our relationships?

HEALING, IN SPITE OF

Our global sisterhood can thrive despite these systems if we are acutely aware of when they are interfering and continue to create and build relationships that will ultimately allow us to create our own systems. It's the duality that comes with just being a Black woman in this world. We must work to dismantle these oppressive systems while simultaneously creating our own systems that allow us space to grow and heal. If we find that we are internalizing racism or misogyny, then we must be willing to be vulnerable to talk about it with our sisters and allow them to help us process why and adjust that programming.

Though these systems exist, there is a way to do our part to minimize damage to both individual sisters and the collective sisterhood. Something that comes up a lot in couples therapy and might be helpful for us is to remember that we are fighting against the problem, not one another. We are fighting white supremacy, not the sister on the job who might not be at her best because of it. We are fighting all the iterations of patriarchy (misogyny and misogynoir, internalized or otherwise), not the sister who bases her entire dating life on the advice from the latest internet guru. We attack the systems, not our sisters. It can be hard to keep sight of that sometimes when our inner stuff gets activated and everybody's upset. But the external issues are the real problem. We are not.

QUESTIONS FOR REFLECTION

1. In what ways have you seen some of these systems impact your relationships with other sisters?

2. When you think about your workplace history, what have the relationships with other Black women been like? Is there something you can do currently to make them better?

3. Of these systems—patriarchy, white privilege, ageism, colorism—which has been the most prevalent issue when you try to connect with other sisters?

4. How might you attempt to be more aware of the ways classism has possibly presented an invisible divide in relationships?

PART III

Tough Times Don't Last Always

Here's to us being afraid and doing it anyway.

—Gabrielle Union

CHAPTER 7

The Intimacy Found in Difficult Conversations

The truth always needs a resting place
or it will lie down wherever it sees fit.

—Tarana Burke

I've spent much of our time together discussing the importance of being and providing safe spaces for one another's humanity. And, yes, while this means holding space for joy and celebration, it also means holding space for the parts of our humanity that aren't always easy to embrace—the more prickly parts, so to speak. Because we are human and not robots, it's inevitable that we will experience situations that can be more difficult to process, which, in turn, can cause tension in our friendships. This book would be five hundred pages long, however, if we tried to capture every single conflict that comes up in sisterhood, including the ones that are just a function of someone saying something rude to somebody else or someone not showing up when they said that they would. But there's a theme that seems to come up repeatedly in my work that does deserve some unpacking. In my observation, the most difficult feelings often arise between sisters when a significant life change—a friend's engagement, a pregnancy, or a career success—disrupts how the relationship has typically functioned.

It's Hard to Be a Friend
and Feel Like a Failure

> I rarely admit it, but when my girlfriends complain about my
> lack of support of them, I know what they are talking about.
> I pretend like I don't, but I do. It's just that they are doing so
> well for themselves. If they aren't rocking out in their profes-
> sional lives, their personal lives are something out of a ro-
> mance novel. And some of them have both. I have neither. I
> don't know what to do with those feelings, so admittedly
> I can come off as unimpressed. It's a defense mechanism, I
> suppose. But I don't know how to celebrate them when my
> life is trash.
>
> —Anna, 26

It is no small feat to be able to admit something this difficult to
ourselves. Many of us have spent a significant amount of time and
energy molding ourselves into versions that are pleasing and pal-
atable to others. But the truth is that feelings like the ones Anna
has shared are normal and valid. Because of who we are as Black
women in this world, it can be easy to believe that good stuff
doesn't happen to or for us. Or it happens rarely. Or it comes with
caveats and/or exhausting hoops to jump through. I've heard
many women share some version of this sentiment. Seeing a sister
obtain the things we might be longing for, in a world that's stingy
anyway, can cause a response that is often shameful for us and
detrimental to our relationships. As Anna has shared, one area
where this plays out in sisterfriendships is in the celebration of
romantic relationships. The idea that your sister has found her
person and you haven't can activate feelings of inadequacy if you
haven't done any work in that area. Of course, you're probably still
happy for your friend, but it might sting. And that pain can cause
you to say or do something hurtful.

One of my friends got engaged in the summer of 2010. She
had been dating her now husband for about two years when the

proposal happened. We all knew the proposal was coming but didn't know exactly when it would be. It was typical for our friend group to get together on Sunday evenings at someone's apartment for dinner and a movie, and on this particular Sunday she wanted to host. That should have been my first sign that something was happening because she doesn't typically like to host, but nonetheless we went about our plans to meet at her home with our assorted goodies at six. The other three sisters in attendance and I were dancing about the apartment, helping to set the table, when she brought out a freshly baked lasagna. That's when I noticed the ring on her finger and squealed at an obnoxious level, calling everyone else's attention to it. This resulted in a chorus of other high-pitched noises and other celebratory gestures. We finally calmed down enough to get the rest of the food on the table and she proceeded to tell us all the details about the proposal.

When we finally stopped pummeling her with questions about the proposal and preliminary plans for the wedding, the friend sitting to the right of me asked, "Are you sure?" I swear you could have heard a pin drop. As the rest of us sat with our mouths slightly agape, our newly engaged friend said, "What do you mean?" This led to a very brief but uncomfortable exchange between them about her readiness to be married and whether her new fiancé was indeed the one. The rest of us tried to revive the vibe by asking more questions about the wedding and awkwardly trying to change the subject, but it was obvious that our engaged friend felt deflated.

At the time, I wondered what would have possessed our friend to ask that question when she did. I mean, yes, getting married is a huge commitment, so checking in with someone you love about their readiness may be something you feel compelled to do. But on the night they announce their engagement? Something about that felt very off. After some time had passed, I asked her about what was going on in that moment, and she shared that because our engaged friend had previously dated someone else for much longer she just wanted to make sure this is what she really wanted.

She didn't realize that it would come across as negatively as it did. She apologized and talked with our friend after the incident, but their relationship has not been quite the same since then.

LIFE CHANGES THAT IMPACT FRIENDSHIPS

I have spent a great deal of time talking with Black women about their relationships with their sisterfriends and have been saddened but not surprised by how many have a story of a friendship ending after one of them got engaged or married. Why is this theme so prevalent?

The biggest culprit is, once again, our socialization. We've been taught to see our friends as placeholders until we find a partner. Common lore says that, in the beginning of a romantic relationship, you're likely to be so invested with your boo that you forget about your girls. We often laugh and joke and normalize this as a good thing. We celebrate it when it's the partner suggesting the time away.

"Oh girl, Toni wants me all to themself. You know how it is."

But let's rethink this for a minute. Is Toni trying to isolate you from your friends? If so, why? Is this a light pink flag we need to be paying attention to? Why can't you spend time with your friends even as you're getting to know this new love interest?

Another part of our socialization as Black women is that some of us are taught that marriage or long-term partnership is the ultimate prize. We are steeped in messaging that tells us that being "chosen" is how our worth and value are validated. Therefore, part of what happens when our sisterfriends become engaged or married and this has not yet happened for us is the activation of some of our earliest experiences of rejection. Those times when parents compared us to older sisters and cousins. Those moments when we were chosen last or not at all for the team. Those suggestions that we'd be perfect if only ___.

A lifetime of being told we're not enough can all come to a head when we see someone else being validated in the ways we long to be. I don't think that much, if any, of this is something we are conscious of in the moment, but just thinking about the significant amount of love, adoration, and consideration our sister will get during the period from engagement to wedding day can call fresh attention to any unhealed wounds we have around not being enough. To deal with the hurt and shame that can come from these feelings, we often do one of two things: (1) We act out in ways that distract from our friend's celebration: *I mean, if I can't have the spotlight, why should she?* Or (2) We push the feelings aside and try to show up for her with a brave face—all while silently harboring resentment that inevitably spills out in other ways.

Not to use another example from the sitcom *Girlfriends* but this dynamic was glaringly obvious when Toni got engaged before Joan. Joan, of course, did the "right" thing and tried to be supportive and excited for her friend but was so overwhelmed by the pain of this not happening for her that she threw herself into running a marathon that she had not trained for and invited her recent ex, Ellis, over to pick up a box of his belongings in the middle of the engagement party that she was hosting for Toni. When Ellis confronted her about this, she initially denied it before succumbing to a tearful rant about being "happy for my friend." In recent discussions about *Girlfriends,* I've heard many women remark on what an awful friend Joan actually was throughout the show and, sure, while she did have some shortcomings, I suspect that some of the disdain for her character is actually because she illustrates some of the shadow sides of ourselves or loved ones that we would rather not acknowledge.

In addition to the feelings of rejection that may be at play when a sisterfriend gets engaged or married, I think that many of us also experience a grief reaction to this change. We don't always realize it, but what's happening for many of us is that we are mourning the relationship we once had with this sister. It's challenging to attach grief to seemingly happy experiences, but that's what happens. It is why we avoid and deny the feelings that come up for us. We know we are supposed to be happy for our girl and her new spouse but mixed in with that happiness is sorrow. Anxiety. Maybe even frustration. It's hard enough acknowledging to ourselves that we feel the way we do; we don't even know if it's okay to admit out loud that these feelings exist. And if it *is* okay, when do we share them? Plus, there are all these ideas out there about how we *should* behave when somebody announces they're engaged—again, socialization—and oftentimes they don't match our internal feelings. We feel worried. We feel scared. We feel sad, angry, or whatever. But that's shameful to say, right? So instead of communicating these feelings at the appropriate time, we act out in ways that create distance in the relationship.

A second life event that often lends itself to subsequent changes in a friendship is pregnancy. Much of the grief response I discussed above also occurs after the announcement of a pregnancy. In this scenario, we are trying to figure out how there will be enough space for sisterhood alongside this new bundle of joy, but an added factor that can certainly color our response is our own fertility history. Handling the news of a sister's pregnancy is often very complex if we've struggled with being able to conceive or carry a child. The duality of being happy for our friend while also being sad that this hasn't happened for us can be a lot to digest at once. And again, socialization makes this more complicated because we are taught that childbearing is what defines us as women and gives us value. Some women cannot see themselves beyond this one thing they are "supposed" to be able to do. Just as rejection wounds get reactivated related to news of an engagement, the wounds of not feeling worthy enough often get activated with the news of a pregnancy.

You've probably noticed a pattern here: Each of these life changes represents something that is exciting and wonderful in one person's life, yet it also changes the dynamic and presents opportunities for us to show up in new and different ways. A third life change that can be challenging to navigate in our friendships is career success. The tension that may arise after a friend gets a new job or a promotion isn't typically about not wanting what's best for her. Sometimes a person's achievement holds up a mirror that shows us the areas where we might not be as successful. Their success can also act as a painful reminder of the risks we didn't or couldn't take that may have led to a new path for us. We also can't forget the systems we discussed in chapter 6 that leave us believing that only one of us can succeed. Even if you and your friend aren't in the same field, that sense of scarcity and feeling of being left behind can be activated by news of her success.

I spoke with one sister who was working through some of these same conflicts in her personal relationships. Fifty-eight-year-old Monica works for a Fortune 500 company and is the only Black woman in a leadership position. She is very intentional about mentoring younger Black women in the space, even though this is often a difficult dynamic for others. She sees it differently, however. While some older Black women might feel threatened by younger people moving into a world they've crafted, Monica is nearing retirement and actively looking for somebody to take her place. The trails she blazed were meant to provide a path for Black women coming up through the ranks. But her biggest challenge was some of the pushback she received within her personal friend circle. When she got her promotion, some of her sisters weren't super supportive. She actually found herself in the position of having to pay for people to come on trips with her just because she wanted the companionship and not because they showed any genuine interest in hanging out with her. Eventually, there was a complete falling-out.

Monica did reveal something in our conversation that was very telling. She said that the promotion was one part of a larger reinvention she was undertaking in her life. She was changing and working on herself and, in many ways, it was a total revamp of who she was before. She'd left an abusive marriage. She'd been deeply active in a church but had begun to shift her thinking about her faith. This is a perfect example of when checking in with ourselves is often necessary before we draw conclusions about how our sisters are feeling about us and our success. I wonder whether Monica considered that her friends may have been struggling with this new version of her, instead of concluding that they weren't supportive of her promotion and career success. The accumulation of changes might have meant that her values were no longer in alignment with theirs. But because no one felt comfortable talking about these feelings, Monica was left feeling hurt and drawing her own conclusions about why things fell apart.

When navigating life changes with our sisterfriends, we must remember that people do change. Personal evolutions happen every day. Sure, a singular shift or change might be something to negotiate or a conflict to heal. But if, like our sister Monica, you transform the entirety of who you are, especially in a short amount of time, it's inevitable that your friends will be confused. And that transformation might necessitate a shift in your circle altogether. You are asking your friends to engage with an entirely different person now. And while we absolutely should allow our friends room to evolve, we also need to be clear when that evolution is in conflict with who we want as a friend going forward.

Here's the thing: No sister should ever be made to feel bad for what she has or has worked hard to attain. I've noticed that some sisters will downplay or shrink their accomplishments in order to not "outshine" their friends. This is not good and, in some cases, can cause more conflict, especially when friends hear about their girl's accomplishments or awards elsewhere and are offended that she didn't say anything.

I've dealt with that personally. Sometimes I don't share what's going on with my work because, well, it's work! I don't want to talk about that with my girls. When I'm with them, I want to relate to them as sisters and friends. I actually want to talk about all the things we usually do and not my upcoming projects or speaking engagements. But I've learned that my friends can feel left out when I don't share. Friends may pull away because they feel excluded and then the sister they are pulling away from is hurt by that and begins making up her own stories about why her friends are not supporting her, and around and around we go. For me and my friends, we are constantly negotiating this dynamic in our relationship and openly communicating about where each of us is.

TELL ME, WHO I HAVE TO BE? TO GET SOME . . .

If you sang along with that heading then you know where I'm going here. When I'm asked what factors indicate a solid friendship, I often lead with *reciprocity*. And while, for the most part, people know what I mean when I use this term, I want to make sure we're working from the same definition here. Reciprocity in relationships refers to all parties feeling like their needs are being met by one another. Reciprocity is not, however, about keeping score. It does not mean that you listened to me vent for an hour this week and so next week I have to listen to you. While that certainly may happen at some point, reciprocity does not imply a one-to-one ratio. In a reciprocal relationship there is no need for an accounting of who did what last because all parties feel like their needs are being met. Everyone feels taken care of and seen in the relationship. I often think that once you find yourself trying to make a list of what you've done for a friend versus what they've done for you, you've likely already crossed the point of no return.

In the TBG community, we've had many discussions about how sisters find themselves in friendships where they are the one always initiating conversations, always responding to crises, always showing up, only to be left on read when they reach out with a concern of their own. If this situation sounds eerily familiar, I want you to think about how the friendship got to this place. Has it always felt one-sided, or is this a more recent development? We've already spent a lot of time talking about some of the life changes that alter the bandwidth we might have for any one area of our lives, so is there a recent change leading them to be less available? Have you tried talking with them about how you're feeling? Even if there is a perfectly understandable reason why they're less available, it's still okay for you to voice your concerns and ask for what you need from the relationship. Likewise, if you've had a recent life change or need some time away from others, if at all possible, let your circle know what's happening. If you don't want to go into detail that's fine, but even a quick text saying "Hey, Sis, I love you and value our relationship but am feeling pretty sad right now and just want some time to feel my way through it. I promise to check in when things feel a little lighter" will help them understand why they're not hearing from you.

And listen, you still deserve to have your needs met in your relationships, so even if friends are able to give you a reason why they can't show up the way you'd like, you still get to decide what feels okay for you. There may be enough history in the relationship that allows for some space and then things just pick up where they left off whenever you come back together. But perhaps it doesn't feel okay to not be supported in the ways you've supported them. In that case, it's also okay to take a step back and redefine what your effort and showing up look like. It may not mean the end of the friendship altogether, but it may mean that it looks very different.

CAN WE TALK?

Open and honest communication is a powerful healer, especially in the case of a long-standing friendship. When big and complicated feelings like the ones we've been talking about come up, it's best not to just sit with them by ourselves; though it may seem counterintuitive, talking about them with the sister involved can often be very helpful. Now I know you may be thinking that there's no way you're going to tell your friend that you think she's jealous of your engagement or that her promotion makes you feel insecure, but many times when we dare to say the hard things, the ugly things, our relationships reach a new level of intimacy and vulnerability that transforms them into an even more restorative and fertile space.

What would it look like to have an honest conversation about envy? The truth is that we aren't "bad people" for feeling envious, even of those who are closest to us. It's what we do afterward that matters. We can act out of our envy and damage our relationships, or we can create space for one another to say, "I'm really happy for you and also wondering when it will be my time." When you think about your closest friends, what would it feel like if one of them came to you and shared that they were happy for your new (insert great thing) and also wondered when it would happen for them? What conditions would need to be met for you to hold space for this exchange? As stated previously, there's a level of emotional intelligence that everyone needs to possess to process these kinds of situations, but my experience has taught me that these types of exchanges can also be very fruitful.

To get the most out of a conversation like this would require that you not internalize their inability to be fully happy for you as being about you (in other words, you couldn't take it personally), and they would have to truly have the courage to give voice to what they're feeling. In this case, the silence would really be the culprit, not the envy.

Hold on now, Sis! Before you send that text saying "we need to talk," I want you to remember that a huge component of having difficult conversations is to be mindful of the timing. It's probably not a good idea to have those conversations about your feelings the same night your friend announces they're engaged or the day she announces her pregnancy or promotion. You don't want to center yourself in someone else's moment. Perhaps wait a week or more, check in with yourself to see how you are feeling to get clarity about what you'd like to discuss, and then broach the subject one-on-one with your friend. Here are some ways you can try to get the conversations started:

If you're worried about how your friend's engagement/marriage will change your friendship:

"Hey, girl! Congratulations again! I just wanted to check in with you about everything that's happening. I'm so very happy for you, and I wanted to be honest with you about how I'm feeling. There's some sadness there also. I suppose I'm worried about how this change in your life will affect our friendship. There's a part of me that doesn't know how things are going to change and I'm anxious about losing you."

And, yes, your friend might say, "Oh girl, you ain't going to lose me!" That's a real response, right? I can totally see one of my girls saying that exact thing. But don't let that deter you. She's not brushing you off. She probably really does believe that everything will be okay. She might not be able to see the challenges from your point of view because she may not have those same feelings. But maybe she does. And maybe she was trying to figure out for herself what this next phase of life might look like. So here's how you might engage her next:

"A part of me knows that. But I think it might be good to talk about how we can continue to have a level of closeness, even as you're embracing this new place in your life. I want to be there for you, but I think I need to know how since I sense it will have to be different from before."

If you're finding it difficult to be happy for your friend's engagement due to your own relationship status:

"Hey, girl! Congratulations again! I just wanted to check in with you about everything that's happening. I'm so happy for you, and it's also been a struggle for me to show up fully because it also makes me sad about not having found my person yet. I'm working through everything that's coming up for me at this moment in our relationship but wanted you to know that it's not a reflection of the joy and excitement I feel for you."

If your friend just had a baby and the relationship has changed:

"I love you and am so happy to see you in this new role as a mom. I'm also really missing you. It seems like it's been forever since we grabbed tacos at our favorite spot. I hope that once you're a little more adjusted to mom life we can figure out some new ways for us to reconnect with each other."

If you're struggling with a friend's pregnancy or recent delivery because of your own fertility struggles:

"Sis, I am so happy for you and the growth of your family. It is so beautiful to watch you become a mom. It's also been a struggle for me

to show up fully because it's a reminder of all the trouble I've had trying to have a baby. I'm working through everything that's coming up for me at this moment in our relationship but wanted you to know that it's not a reflection of the joy and excitement I feel for you."

If you're struggling with the news of a friend's career success:

"Sis, I'm so glad that you are finally getting your due. I'm so proud of you. I have to admit, though, that I'm also frustrated because I haven't been able to have that kind of success in my own life. Are there things you can share that might help me get to the next level in my career?"

If you are the person who is experiencing the life change and having this conversation with a friend, I invite you to not dismiss their sharing with you. Amid planning a life with a partner or beginning the journey of parenting, your attention will rightfully be in another place. But to maintain all your relationships—not just the one with your partner or children—it's always good to consider how others around you might be feeling. While you might not be able to or want to change what's happening in your life, it's compassionate to check in with people to understand why they are or are not okay. Ask yourself if it's possible to slow down just a beat to have these kinds of loving conversations with your sisterfriends. You might not come to a resolution. Both of you might end up saying, "It is what it is." But there's power in listening to our sisters. Can you hear when your sister is sad? Can your sister hear your joy? All without taking things personally? Remember, it's rarely about not being happy for you. It's often about making sense of the complex emotions we have as human beings. Here is some language that might be helpful for you:

If you just had a baby and notice something off with a friend:

"I know you love me and the baby. And I see that you might be having some complicated feelings around where this leaves us. I'm pretty sleep deprived so I don't have all the answers right now, but I love you and want to figure out how we can reconnect when I feel a little more steady. I just need some time to navigate this new world I'm in."

If you've noticed a change in a friend since your engagement or wedding:

"Hey! I just wanted to check in with you. It feels like something's been off ever since I got engaged/married. I know this is a huge change for all of us. Is there anything you want to check in about?"

If you just announced a pregnancy or had a baby and know a friend is struggling because of her fertility concerns:

"I'm so grateful we've been able to be in each other's corners through so many seasons of our lives. I know that so much has changed/will change with the new baby and imagine some of this may be really difficult for you. I know you love me and the baby and want you to know that there is space in our friendship for both of our experiences."

If you suspect a friend is struggling with your career success:

"I'm so excited about this new opportunity in my life, but I've noticed that there's been some distance since I announced my promotion. Is there something we can check in about? I want us all to win so if there's anything I can do to help you, I will."

Remember that the suggestions I've laid out here are just that—suggestions. The words may not be the ones you'd use, so feel free to revise as needed. The point is to be able to directly acknowledge that something has shifted in your relationship and create a space for compassion and curiosity. Before initiating any of these conversations, it's important to do some work on your own to make sure you're clear about what is coming up for you related to this change. If you have a therapist or are interested in talking with a therapist, this would be a great issue to bring to your sessions to help you understand what's being activated in you by your friend's new life experience or what may be going on in your relationships as your life changes.

So how do we make room for and accept the life changes we are all bound to experience in some shape or form, the spectrum of emotions that will show up as we navigate this life together, but sustain our intimate love interest relationships with our girl-friends?

Bottom line: We choose to be intentional.

Your sisterfriendships shouldn't just be important to you until you obtain these other markers (partnership, job success, parenthood) in your life. Sisterhood is always our safe place. So even if it doesn't look the same, it's important to create space in your life for the people you love and who matter. So let's have the difficult conversations with one another. I know that it feels easier to avoid difficult conversations out of fear of abandonment or the belief that our sisters are going to hate us. We think being open is going to damage our relationships when in actuality the hard conversations can draw true friends closer. You are able to unlock a new level of transparency and vulnerability in the relationship. The irony is that the intimacy we so desperately want is on the other side of that conversation we're avoiding.

Truthfully, these kinds of dynamics in our sisterhoods are an ongoing negotiation. We may even have to come back and check in with our friends periodically. Nevertheless, it's critical to remind ourselves that, as much as possible, we should try not to personalize other people's feelings and behaviors. The way people respond or react to us and what's going on in our lives is most often a reflection of them and their stuff, not us or their feelings about us. Being able to see things clearly for what they are can help to cut down on misunderstandings and hard feelings.

QUESTIONS FOR REFLECTION

1. What have been your experiences with feeling rejected? How does it typically show up in your relationships? Is there anything you feel like you need to do differently to manage it?

2. Is there a difficult conversation you're currently avoiding? What are you worried might happen? What's the best thing that could come from having the conversation?

What's the worst thing that could happen if you continue to avoid the conversation?

3. How do you and your sisters typically navigate life changes? Is there anything that could be done differently to create a space of more compassion and curiosity?

CHAPTER 8

The Life Stages of Our Circles

Walls turned sideways are bridges.

–Angela Davis

If you've been in a sister circle long enough, it's likely that the group has gone through several different stages. There was the very beginning where you were all getting to know one another and feeling one another out. You know, the "Hey, Girl, Hey" stage where things are light and the group chat is mostly fun memes and questions about the latest binge watch. Then you moved to the phase of deeper conversations and connections, where you all weren't just casual anymore. Finally, there may have been a major event, perhaps someone became ill or moved away, and the group had to reorganize to make space for this new reality. You all worked through that beautifully, and now you're pretty much coasting along. Yes, I know this is a very idealized version of what these stages might look like, but the point is that your sister circle today probably looks very different from the way it did during the first year of its existence, and lots of things have shaped it into its current form. This transformation occurs in group therapy as well.

In group therapy, there are expected stages that groups go through as they develop, including forming, storming, norming, and performing. Forming refers to the process of everyone getting to know one another, feeling out the space, and trying to figure

out their role in the group as well as how this space might be useful to them. This is often seen as the "polite" stage of group development. In the storming stage, members begin to experience
more conflict with one another as they try to navigate the space
together. We see things like jockeying for control, and competition issues surface. Members experience the most discomfort at
this stage, but it is critical for the group's success because the work
of healing with one another cannot happen unless the group is
able to learn how to navigate conflict, which is what leads to a
sense of cohesion and belonging for the members. In the norming
stage, things begin to regulate as members develop a sense of how
this space works for everyone. A clear flow for how time is spent
together is developed, and members feel safe to take more risks
with one another. The performing stage is the working stage of a
group, where most of the changes happen for members. Members
rely easily on one another, and there is a clear sense of purpose for
the group.

While our sister circles don't necessarily follow these same
stages of development, there are definitely shifts in the dynamics
of our circles as we experience various life situations both as individuals and as a collective. These include the introduction of new
friends into the circle, weddings, personal financial values, loss,
and sickness. We'll dig deeper into each of these areas in this chapter, but let's make sure we are cognizant of the source of some of
our challenges.

THE IMPACT OF OUR CHILDHOOD STORIES

Are you back at our childhoods again, Dr. Joy? I know, I know. But,
yes, our childhood experiences can definitely impact how we
move within our sister circles without our recognizing it. If we
grew up never feeling like we were enough or like we always had
to "do the most" to be seen and valued for whatever reason, then
it's likely that you will show up that way in all of your relationships, including with your sisters. Feelings of not being enough
might reveal themselves as jealousy because you have created a

story that centers you as the character who never receives good things because you're not good enough. I encourage you to be on the lookout for the things that keep showing up in your relationships because it's highly likely that they're the things connected to your own personal work.

People don't generally arrive at the recognition of their childhood wounds without some form of therapy. If you know these things about yourself, I recommend sharing these childhood wounds with your close sisterfriends so that when your behavior begins to line up with how these issues tend to manifest, they might be able to gently remind you of the work you are doing to heal. And if a friend is not able to be vulnerable enough to share, the sister circle can still have a conversation about what's showing up and where it might be coming from. For instance, jealousy generally reveals itself as passive-aggressive behavior and petty comments. Neglect might manifest as resentment and accidentally missing important events. Abandonment issues might show up as co-dependent behavior, which could lead to constant texting, or calling, or showing up unannounced.

In fact, the traumatic childhood experience that seems to have the largest impact on friendships is abandonment. It's the feeling that people are going to leave us at any time and we don't have control over it. As a result, sisters who struggle with abandonment issues often show up in their relationships with people-pleasing behavior. As noted, they tend to be needy and/or clingy. They also tend to be the biggest proponents of the "no new friends" mantra, not because they don't want more intimacy in their sister circle but because they believe that bringing in new people might mean they are less important in the group.

There are also the kinds of childhood events that aren't necessarily rooted in neglect and abuse but still have an impact on how we move as adults. If a sister grew up in poverty, she may struggle with spending money for a girls' trip, not because she really doesn't have it, but because she hasn't reconciled her mindset around money and lack. Having friends who understand this and don't shame her for it is invaluable.

Is There Still Room for Me?

I've been so used to it just being me and my girls—the three of us who went to high school and college together—that I'm having a very hard time dealing with the fact that one of my friends has started inviting this chick she works with, Tasha, to all our get-togethers. I mean, she's cool or whatever. I don't necessarily have any beef with her. But I feel some kind of way because I don't know her. She doesn't know me like they do. And I feel like she hasn't been vetted in the way that we have each other over the years. I'm hesitant to talk as candidly as I would ordinarily and it just feels awkward. Sometimes I just cancel because I can't deal with it. But then I feel angry when they meet up anyway because it seems like Ms. Tasha is going to take my spot.

—Shawnna, 32

There's a lot to wade through in what Shawnna shared here. First of all, I know that she is not alone in feeling like the way you prepare for a night out with your girls when you know it's just going to be y'all versus when "company" is coming is *very* different. I often get a hearty chuckle when I see various versions of this conversation online because it's real. Underlying the concerns about not feeling like she can be as open and candid when Tasha is around is the sincere worry about whether her spot in the circle is somehow threatened by the presence of Tasha. Believe it or not, this is one of the common sister circle challenges I've heard from clients in therapy as well as in conversations with the larger TBG community.

Expanding the Circle

New friends entering the circle can often be tricky to deal with. Circles that have been formed for a while, like the one Shawnna is a part of, tend to have a flow to them that can be easily upset by the introduction of new members. This doesn't mean we shouldn't expand our circles. It simply means we should be mindful about how it's done. To begin with, there needs to be a conversation with other members about what's happening. In Shawnna's case, it doesn't appear that her friend checked in before she just started inviting Tasha to hang out with them.

Now perhaps this friend thinks that the rest of the group will love Tasha when they get to know her better, but this is less likely if she's not been invited into the group with intention. Instead of just assuming everyone will be cool with it, perhaps Shawnna's friend could have talked to the others in the group and said something like "Hey! I work with this really cool sister Tasha, and I think you'd both really like her. She's hilarious. Would it be okay if I invited her out to dinner with us on Friday?" This would have given the group a heads-up and allowed them to voice any concerns they may have about someone else joining. Now listen, I know some folks might be thinking that they wouldn't want to rock the boat, so they'd probably say yes to letting Tasha join anyway, even if they felt a way about it, but vulnerability and authenticity are what we've spent a lot of time talking about here, so I want to gently encourage you to consider that if a sister asks a similar question of you at some point . . . be honest with her. It's perfectly okay to say something like "I'm sure Tasha's great, but I really just want time with the two of you this week."

Another part of being intentional about inviting others into your circle—as was illustrated in Shawnna's story—is that the introduction of new members often activates a sense of being replaced or forgotten by others. Remember those attachment styles we talked about in chapter 1? They're important to consider when we talk about expanding our circles to include new people. Sisters who have an insecure attachment style based on their early experiences with parents and other caregivers are more likely to feel like they need to hold tightly to relationships or else they will end. They are often afraid that if their friend likes this other person too much, the friend won't need them any longer. These are the sisters in the circle who will be most resistant to expanding it. There's a strong possibility that our sister circles are comprised of sisters with various types of attachment styles, so in thinking about adding a new member to the group, it's important to be in tune with how everyone will be impacted. While a sister with a more secure attachment may be all for someone new joining, someone with a more insecure attachment will likely struggle with this.

Once again, we see that our sister circle dynamics mimic those found in therapy groups: Introducing someone new into a therapy group often stirs up a lot of feelings in current members. It's not uncommon for those in the group to be angered by the presence of a new person because they think that the attention will shift to the newbie, or they don't trust the new person because they haven't invested the same amount of time and vulnerability as the other members. As we unpack these issues in the therapeutic setting, we usually find that some type of attachment injury from early life has been awakened, which provides a golden opportunity to discuss how this still impacts them and to do some great work in creating a plan to navigate it. Our sister circles can also provide some safety but only if these conversations are introduced and we are intentional before expanding the circle. A million different conflicts can show up in a sister circle, but here are a few that come up time and time again in my work that I'd like to walk us through.

DIFFERENCES IN VALUES

There are things we may not know about a member of our circle until a particular situation presents itself. This was definitely the case during the pandemic. I heard from many sisters that they were shocked and at times disappointed in some of the things they learned about friends, including their willingness or not to mask, their beliefs about vaccines, and their sentiments toward public health. Against the backdrop of such a monumental experience, it became very difficult for many sisters to navigate relationships with people they were very close to but felt very distant from at the same time. While this pandemic example may be extreme, sometimes differences in values impact cohesiveness in a circle.

One way to attempt to navigate these differences is by suspending judgment until there is an opportunity for everyone to be heard. It is very easy for us to assign meaning to someone else's behavior when it's different from our own, but in close relationships, allowing our friends to tell us more about what's driving their behaviors can help us to figure out how that behavior and the values associated with it land within the confines of the friendship. We can agree to disagree on some differences, but there are other values, perhaps the ones that are core to us, that do not leave any room for differences. If you realize that the difference is one that you can agree to disagree on, perhaps you tread lightly around that topic in an effort to preserve the friendship. However, if after a conversation where everyone is given the opportunity to be heard, you realize that your values about a particular area simply don't mesh, it is okay to end the friendship at this point rather than to dishonor yourself, further strain the relationship, or compromise your values.

WEDDING SEASON

I've already discussed how the dynamics of our friendships can shift on an individual basis after someone in a sister circle gets engaged or married, but there is also a particular experience related to wedding planning that occurs within the sister circle as a whole. Some of those same early experiences of rejection and not being enough can be activated as the bride chooses what role, if any, members of the sister circle will play in the bridal party. Because brides themselves are acting out the same early experiences of rejection or inadequacy, the behavior that results places a significant strain on the relationships within the circle. For example, there can be a great deal of tension surrounding who is chosen to be maid/matron of honor and whether or not one or all of the group will be chosen as bridesmaids. For the potential bridesmaid, this placement may signify an indication of the importance they play in the bride's life, and for the bride it may be an opportunity to garner validation and attention that feels more socially appropriate. Another source of tension revolves around what is expected of the bridal party. This, of course, differs for every celebration, but it is not uncommon these days for a wedding season to consist of an engagement party, a bachelorette party, a bridal luncheon, the wedding day, and a farewell brunch. Each of these events may require travel, special outfits, and expenses. It can be very easy to end up spending a significant amount of time and money in an effort to show up for a friend; there is also the potential for tension if or when a friend needs to legitimately opt out. Here are some things to consider if your circle is embarking on a wedding season.

For the Bride

What feelings come up for you when you think about how you want this season to look? Does it excite you to have all eyes on you and your partner? Does that feel uncomfortable? When you think about the events and plans you're setting in motion for this season, what are you hoping to accomplish? What story are you telling yourself about how you will feel during this time? About how you will be perceived? And how do you want others to feel? The excitement of planning an event where many of the people who mean the most to us will be in attendance can be invigorating, but it can also awaken little wounds that we thought were healed and even some we didn't know existed. Before the planning goes too far, spend some time getting clear about what you want and how you want to feel at this time.

You must also consider how you want your circle to feel. Yes, it is an opportunity for you to be celebrated but that doesn't mean that others need to feel antagonized in the process. We've already talked quite a bit about what our socialization as Black women teaches us about getting married, so there's a good chance you've been thinking about what this time in your life would look like for a long time. With this kind of buildup comes many expectations that often go unvoiced. Be clear with your circle about how you would like them involved during this time and also be sensitive to the fact that, depending on what is asked, they may not be able to be involved exactly the way you would like. This is probably not an indication of their love for you or a measure of their level of excitement about this time in your life.

Additionally, be mindful of what's driving your decision-making about what this time in your life looks like. We discussed earlier how this is often a time that warrants a great deal of adoration and attention, and if you are someone who thrives in the spotlight, it may be great. But if you're someone who has been purposely kept out of the spotlight, the same type of adulation may feel not only very welcome but also intoxicating, so you need to be careful not to misuse those you love and who love you as a result.

For the Supporting Sisters

Be mindful of the ways that socialization may be impacting your friend's behavior during this time and also be okay with setting boundaries to honor yourself. There may be some asks made of you during this time that seem completely reasonable to her but are completely unreasonable to you. It is okay to say no and mean it while also being very excited to honor her. As I always say, be aware of what is coming up for you. Earlier we discussed why this may be a difficult time in a circle, so pay attention to what's coming up for you and find spaces outside of the circle to share how you're feeling and to get support for yourself. Understand that many of the decisions being made by your friend have little to do with her love and care for you and are likely a reflection of internal and external pressure she may be experiencing. Create spaces to connect with her that have nothing to do with wedding planning, as this can often be a welcome respite.

MONEY, MONEY, MONEY!

You're likely very familiar with any number of adages that warn against mixing finances and friends. We've been discouraged from talking about how much we make with our friends, warned against borrowing from or loaning money to friends, and dissuaded from hiring friends in our businesses or starting ventures together. As is often the case with topics that can be polarizing or where things can get sticky, one of the best ways to take some of the flame from a fire is to be clear with expectations.

One area where I often see difficulties in sister circles as it relates to money is around borrowing and loaning money. Sisters tend to be either very much on the "if I have it, it's yours" side or firmly on the "please don't ask" side. There isn't necessarily a right or wrong camp; it all comes down to how these differences around money are discussed. For this reason, if possible, I think it's helpful to talk about this as a circle before the need arises. How does everyone feel about asking to borrow money? Would some members be okay loaning money while others might not be? How would the dynamic be impacted by someone asking for a loan and then being told no? How would the circle respond to someone experiencing a clear need but not being comfortable to ask even if there were some members willing to offer the loan? These are all great places to start.

What you don't want to happen is for there to be an ask and then a rupture because no one is actually comfortable lending money. I also think it's important to add that not wanting to loan money isn't necessarily about a lack of trust; it may have more to do with a person's own relationship to money than it has to do with not believing you will pay them back. If you are someone who is okay with offering a loan to a friend, please consider lending only what you can afford to not get back. Even with the best intentions, things happen and unfortunately there are times when loans are not repaid. If you can afford to offer it as a gift, that may be even better because then there is no expectation of being paid back. Should you be in a situation where you have accepted a loan and now realize that you won't be able to repay it according to plan, consider letting your friend know this as soon as possible and offer to make smaller payments in hopes that at some point this might change. The worst thing you can do in this situation is to avoid the topic and pretend that the loan wasn't ever given. People can often work with us through a tough spot;

it is far more difficult to repair a relationship after trust has been undermined. Take whatever steps you can to maintain the trust that exists.

And as you contemplate and discuss these questions, remember that even with the best of intentions, we know that things can happen. I've always believed it best to consider loaning only what you can afford not to be paid back. If there's any suspicion that the circle could be ruptured by a loan that is not paid back, it may be a better strategy to help the sister explore other options.

ATTENDING TO A FRIEND'S GRIEF

If our circle exists for long enough, there will undoubtedly be a time when the group is focused on supporting someone through the loss of a loved one. When that happens, it can be hard to know what to do or say, and the mistake we often make is not saying or doing anything. We worry that asking about the deceased loved one will only make the memories more painful and instead choose to avoid these conversations. Oftentimes there is nothing further from the truth. Asking a friend to share memories and stories about their loved one can be comforting and sends the message that you understand how important this person was to them and that you are holding space for them to remember.

Understanding that we all grieve differently is key. Some people isolate and want solitude while others throw themselves into a project. This is especially important when discussing Black women because we've not historically been given space to be sad and grieve, so your sister might find herself doing the thing that comes naturally—throwing herself into work or a new project. And while some level of distraction may help to manage the intensity of grief, it might also prevent her from tending to herself in the way that is needed following a loss. I invite us as friends of someone grieving not to be fooled by this performance of okayness and to be gentle but intentional about helping our Sis make space for her grief. In addition to that intentionality, here are a few other things to consider:

- She may not know what she needs. Many times, our go-to when someone is grieving is to say "let me know what you need." But the truth is that grieving people often don't know what they need. As much as possible, the circle should try to anticipate some of her needs. Prep or deliver meals to make sure she has food. Go over to the house and wash dishes or a load of clothes. Offer to help her make arrangements, if necessary. Be there to let her cry or offer to sleep over so that she's not alone at night if she lives by herself.

- Attend the services. Funerals and other memorials can be very uncomfortable to attend, but if at all possible, try to be there. Friends often see this as a very concrete way of your being there during a time when they needed it most. If you can't be in attendance, see if it's possible to send a flower arrangement or offer to help with the repast if one is scheduled.

- Don't assume she's not still grieving in six weeks or six months. Many bereaved people have commented that they find the months after a funeral or memorial service the most difficult because they often feel forgotten. Many of the house visits and meal offers have stopped and they are alone with their thoughts. Be intentional about showing up after all the activity has come to a stop. Put reminders on your calendar to check in and make a note to remember the death anniversary as this will likely be a difficult time of the year for her. It would be great for the circle to offer a little extra care and support as the anniversary gets closer.

In Sickness and in Health

Similar to the experience of losing a loved one, a sister in the circle experiencing an illness can be equally destabilizing. This can be complicated because Black women tend to keep health concerns to themselves for fear of worrying or being a burden to others. But for those circles where this information is shared, there are some tangible ways to show support for this sister.

- Offer to go to doctor's visits with her. Sometimes when people are experiencing a health crisis it can be difficult to fully comprehend what healthcare professionals are sharing. If this is the case, offer to attend to help take notes for her to review later and to ask any questions that may seem important. If this isn't the case, you can still offer to be there, even if only in the waiting room, for moral support.
- Don't pretend like there's nothing happening. You may be feeling like you're making her health too much of a focus by asking questions and checking in with her, but the alternative is to make her feel like you don't care and that this is too big for the circle to hold. Trust that she will set limits with you if she'd like the focus to be elsewhere as opposed to assuming otherwise.
- Help her find additional support. The process of finding a specialized therapist or other healthcare professional can be daunting. Try to help with the search by doing some research for professionals who meet her criteria and offer a shorter list that she can then choose from.
- Find out if there's a way the group can support her health. Does she need to cut back on sugar to improve her out-comes? Perhaps more physical activity is needed? Consider ways the group can support this by taking a class in low-sugar cooking together or going on evening walks.

When a Friend Is Depressed or Struggling with Their Mental Health

We often hear the refrain to "check in on your strong friends" after a high-profile person dies by suicide or reveals they are struggling with their mental health. While these calls for action are often well intentioned, it is not always clear what one is to do as part of this "check in." When we know this sister we love is struggling, our initial response is often the same one we use for other types of grief: "Let me know if there's anything I can do to help." While perhaps thoughtful, those sentiments typically do not go far enough for someone who is depressed or struggling in a similar way.

One of the hallmark symptoms of a depressive disorder is a difficulty with concentration and other executive functioning. This means they may not be able to organize their thoughts well enough to let you know what they need. If possible, try to anticipate what they may need. Offer to do very practical things that might make a big difference, like going over to wash dishes or do a load of laundry. People who are depressed often have a loss of appetite or no motivation to feed themselves, so consider bringing over their favorite food or some protein shakes/smoothies in case it's easier for them to get something down by drinking rather than chewing. Something else that can be helpful and comforting for people struggling with mental health challenges is for you to just be present while they do something they may want or need to do, but can't find the motivation to start. Simply standing in a doorway, talking to them from the hallway, may give them the extra push they need to take a shower or wash their hair.

Similarly, they may not want you to talk. Perhaps just being there to sit with them while they take a nap would be comforting. Supporting someone struggling with their mental health can look lots of different ways and oftentimes tailoring your attempts to help comes down to what you know about your sisters and how they tend to be impacted when they're struggling. I recently saw a post shared via *Today* that beautifully captured what it can look like to show up for someone we love when they're having a hard time. After Ashlee experienced a miscarriage, her friend Anna sent the following text as a way of checking in on her.

Checking on you. Please choose from the following:

1.) I pick your kids up any time after 3:30 today & show them a good time through dinner (which would be at Chick-fil-A, obvi, & would include takeout brought back for you).

2.) I send DoorDash dinner of your choice to you. (This offer is valid any day this week. Also next week.)

3.) I have to go to Target today, I can pick up anything you need & drop it on your doorstep & not talk to you at all.

4.) I can send prayers & good vibes & you can politely decline any tangible services at this time.[1]

This is wonderful! Offering options that involve both tangible and intangible things, silence or presence, is a great model to adopt when we consider how we might offer support to a sister who may be struggling with her mental health, and one that would likely be appreciated and helpful.

Longevity within a sister circle is often a blessing, and it also means that you've likely experienced some significant life stuff together. Research indicates that having a strong support system is a significant factor in being able to rebound following a life stressor. To ensure that our systems stay intact, it is important to know how to effectively navigate conflicts that may arise and how to support one another through difficult experiences.

QUESTIONS FOR REFLECTION

1. In your longest-existing sister circle, how does your relationship look different now from when it began? What kinds of things have helped you all navigate the various stages you've experienced?

2. How did your sister circle navigate the pandemic? Did any tension arise due to differences of opinion? Did anything surprise you about your circle during this time?

3. If you were struggling with your mental health, what do you imagine your sister circle could offer that might be most helpful and comforting? It might be a great idea to discuss this question with your circle so that you can all hear one another's suggestions/ideas/offers.

CHAPTER 9

Quite Possibly the Worst Heartbreak: When Sisterhood Ends

You've got to learn to leave the table
when love's no longer being served.

—Nina Simone

In her groundbreaking text *Black Feminist Thought,* Dr. Patricia Hill Collins states that Black women must study Black women because only they can ask the critical questions about themselves. Only we intimately know the interiors of one another's worlds. Sadly, this is also why betrayals and disappointments by our sisters cut the deepest and why the loss of a sisterfriendship feels so devastating. When a relationship with a sister ends, especially if it's someone we have known for any significant length of time, it is incredibly painful. The space in our hearts that used to be filled by this person who loved us and whom we loved is now empty, and that void is, at the very least, an emotional disruption.

Sometimes these relationships end and there is a "thing" to point to. Other times, the friendship ends as a natural course of the relationship's life span. Endings don't always have to be loud and dramatic; now and then they are quiet and unassuming. The dissolution of a friendship doesn't have to mean there is animosity or that anyone is "bad." Sometimes things have just run their course. Perhaps you are now just loving each other from a distance. Maybe you've done your personal work, had the difficult conversations I encouraged you to have, and still can't come to a resolution when there is conflict. Whatever has happened, these endings impact us in myriad ways and care must be taken in their aftermath.

IT'S HARD TO ACCEPT THAT IT'S OVER

> We had been friends for forever. She'd seen me through a marriage, two children, a divorce, career changes, health challenges, and more. And, yes, maybe there were little signs along the way. Things that we ignored because of our history. She was changing and so was I. And I guess those changes caused us to grow apart. But I still never thought our friendship would end completely. The idea that I can't call her, that things are not the same, well, I'm having a hard time accepting that.
>
> —Constance, 45

Unfortunately, the experience that Constance shared is one many of us know all too well. The thing that makes friendship breakups so difficult, especially the ones where there's no real precipitating event to point to, is that we have typically created these very intimate worlds with one another. We have our own language and way of engaging that's ours alone. We know our sisters' secrets. So when a friendship ends, that whole world ceases to exist. It hurts to know that no one holds sacred those personal stories anymore. There's no one to laugh at the inside jokes we had anymore. As much as we are grieving the loss of the person, we are also grieving the world we created together that can no longer exist. Not to mention the weight of perhaps having to find new sisterfriends. There's so much that our current friends know about us, issues they know how to navigate. It can be hard to imagine having to do that again.

A particular type of devastation occurs when the person who is typically there to help you put the pieces back together is the reason they shattered in the first place. We are often left grieving when close friendships end. However, society often respects grief only if it is related to the death of a loved one. In actuality, many different types of losses can trigger grief: the loss of a job, the loss of an ability, the loss of a dream that has been held for a long time. These are referred to as non-death losses. The type of grief that is experienced with non-death losses like the loss of a friendship, the loss of an opportunity, etc., is called disenfranchised grief. Disenfranchised grief is not recognized as valid or real and often does not carry the same customs and rituals that are experienced after the loss of a loved one. Because the same weight and reverence is not typically offered in the case of disenfranchised grief, it can be difficult for those experiencing it to fully process their grief.

In season 4 of HBO's *Insecure,* the two main characters, Issa Dee and Molly Carter, experience a slow and painful end to their yearslong friendship after a series of life events and hurtful exchanges. This was one of the few times a Black television show had so deeply explored a friendship breakup, and it struck a nerve with the TBG community. We even spent several episodes of the podcast dissecting and unpacking what was happening in their relationship. For as much joy as Black women can find in one another, there also exists the potential for a gutting, all-encompassing pain, especially when a relationship with a sister ends or when we are hurt by a sister. I believe that *Insecure* struck a chord with our community because there is not typically a lot of space in pop culture or otherwise given to the relationships between Black women, and this was one of the first opportunities for us to see ourselves in this way on a popular show. And even though by the end of *Insecure,* Issa and Molly found their way back to each other, all of us know that's not something that happens all the time.

I inevitably run into the question of how long we should work to salvage a relationship. How many hard conversations do we have before we cut our losses and distance ourselves from a sister? Well, there's no easy answer. There's no schedule that says after five or six or ten conversations, it's over. It's an individual determination based on what we are willing to do to maintain what might not be working. Usually there's an internal knowing that will show up and make us aware when to let go, combined with a series of emotions that come up when we're in a person's presence. Maybe you're not looking forward to spending time with them anymore, or the thought of spending time with them makes you feel anxious. Maybe when you see their name pop up in your text messages or phone, you don't feel inclined to respond. These are just a few signs that it may not be a fruitful relationship for you anymore. It's entirely possible that it doesn't provide the kind of nurturing for you that it had in the past. If you've done the work to make sure that you haven't built a story about that person that isn't actually true, then it's possible that the relationship is ending and it's time for you to grieve what once was.

When to Say When

What confuses us about friendship breakups is that we don't expect to experience the same symptoms of grief that we would feel in relation to any other loss. We feel silly or become hypercritical of ourselves, saying things like "Is it really that big of a deal?" The answer is an unequivocal yes! Some of the classic symptoms of grief are loss of concentration, difficulty with motivation, not really being interested in much, and isolating yourself. These are some of the things we also see in those of us who are grieving the loss of a friendship.

There are three areas where we will primarily find ourselves grieving a relationship with our sisters. First, maybe that life change mentioned earlier results in long periods of physical distance that cause you to grow apart (the global pandemic is an example of this) or there is an emotional distance that has happened because of philosophical/political impasses (the polarization that can come with sociopolitical beliefs). Finally, significant, unresolved conflict surfaces after a betrayal or after something traumatic in our lives happens and our friend(s) don't know how to be our friend anymore.

In the case of physical or emotional distance as a result of growing apart or a philosophical shift, sometimes it just is what it is. The relationship has run its course, and the grieving process is really more about dealing with what it means to let go. When we know a relationship is ending, we need to talk to our sisters and express what we are feeling.

Goodbyes are not something we do well in this society. When relationships are painful, too many of us just leave. We ghost each other. We stop taking our sister's calls or quietly exit the group chat. We often use these types of avoidance tactics because we are afraid of having difficult and awkward conversations or we feel unskilled at how to initiate them. In an article for the *Washington Post,* Dr. Royette Dubar recounts the observations of a study she conducted on college campuses. The study ultimately found that ghosting is so common nowadays because many people lack either the "necessary communication skills to have an open and honest conversation" or the confidence to confront whatever conflict may be present. She also noted that "ghosting can have negative consequences for mental health. Short term, many of those ghosted felt overwhelming rejection and confusion. They reported feelings of low self-worth and self-esteem. . . . Long term, [the] study found many of those ghosted reported feelings of mistrust that developed over time. Some bring this mistrust to future relationships."[1]

In our sisterfriendships we are too often hoping that if we just fall off the surface that our sisters will get the message. However, unless there has been harm perpetrated or danger in engaging with a person, having the difficult conversation about the ending of a friendship is actually a way for us to honor what was. It's a way of saying even though this didn't turn out to be a best-friend-for-life kind of thing, it was still significant. *I still care.* It also gives the other person clarity. It's a kindness we offer our sisters in being clear about opting out of the relationship. It's also a kindness to ourselves, as the anxiety we experience as we anticipate what this conversation may be like is often far more intense than if we had the actual conversation.

I've spoken to many sisters who felt more devastated by the ghosting of a best friend than by the ending of the relationship itself. They wanted to have that difficult conversation because they believed all parties owed it to one another to say goodbye.

I've also spoken with women who chose not to have a breakup conversation, mainly because they didn't have the language for it. So let me help you with that. Here are some words you might use to begin the breakup talk:

"It feels difficult to say this, but I feel like I'm no longer getting what I need from our friendship, and I think it's best to end things here. I'm grateful for the time we've spent together and wish you nothing but the best moving forward."

Now listen, this is not likely to be an easy pill to swallow for your friend, especially if she doesn't see it coming. It's important for you to remember why you're ending it and to not be swayed by her attempts to pull you back in. You've likely given it lots of thought and it's important to be clear with how you're feeling. She will likely be hurt by the ending of the friendship, just like you're probably going to be left with some hurt even though you're the one ending it. But being honest and upfront about how you're feeling is ultimately the kindest thing you can do for both of you.

Some of these same grief symptoms will certainly show up in relationships that end because of major conflict or betrayal. But one of the emotions we might have to contend with in betrayal that may not be present in other scenarios is anger. If a friendship falls apart because of distance or because we believe different things, then there's usually sadness and maybe emptiness and despair about what will no longer be. But if my sister betrays me in some way, then I'm also being forced to reconcile my love for her with my rage at what she's done. Not to mention that because of the intensity of that kind of loss, I will know that the ending of the relationship will impact more than just me. If she slept with my partner, then now I have to deal with the potential loss of two relationships. If she was the godmother to my children, I have to reckon with the impact her absence will have on my children.

So how does one reconcile the grief and anger happening at the same time in this kind of friendship breakup?

Slowly. Very slowly.

Don't make any drastic decisions too soon after the end. Give yourself time to move through all those emotions. It can be difficult to think logically when there's so much going on. Lean on a good support system, sisters who can help you navigate what you are feeling.

She WAS my support, Dr. Joy!

I get it. That's the hardest part of this kind of loss—when your sister was your person, the one who supported you in every area of your life, and now you don't have her to go to. It's painful and yet you will still need to reach out to somebody who can stand alongside you in this grieving process. Someone who is not going to make you feel silly for the sorrow and anger and anything else that comes up because your sister has betrayed you.

HOW TO LET GO

As I mentioned before, the loss of a sisterfriend is often painful, and the grief that we endure must be tended to. You may be most familiar with the five stages of grief proposed by psychiatrist Elisabeth Kübler-Ross—denial, anger, bargaining, depression, and acceptance—which she believed people experienced after the loss of a loved one.[2] Many scholars in the field of death and dying have expanded our understanding of what happens when we are grieving to go beyond these stages to reflect a more fluid experience of grieving. The dual process model of coping with bereavement explains that we move through grieving by oscillating between confronting the loss and avoiding it.[3] This model of bereavement has also been adapted to be used to help us understand what grief looks like as it relates to non-death losses. The model suggests that against the backdrop of everyday life we alternate between thoughts and feelings that focus on the loss and those that help us to rebuild a life after the loss.[4]

When breaking up in a romantic context, sisters often talk about "needing closure." It stands to reason that we would also want closure in our friendship breakups. But here's the thing, Sis: Closure doesn't come from other people. It comes from us making peace with the reality that this thing we loved has ended—whether we get that final "goodbye" conversation or not.

Often after the end of a friendship we are left with lots of questions and very few answers. Our desire for closure may result in us making attempts to reach out to our former friend in hopes that they will be able to say something, anything, to lessen the pain. It is normal and expected, but it is not effective. Believing that someone else will be able to string together just the right words to make us feel better only leaves us holding our healing hostage, waiting for someone else to release us. Rituals or setting boundaries can be a good way for you to release everything you might want to say in a closure conversation without the confrontation. Here are a few self-care practices that may help you to tend to yourself in your quest to achieve closure.

Write a Letter

Try writing a letter to your former friend asking all the questions you wish you had the answers to and sharing how the end of this friendship has left you feeling. Name all the things you are angry about and anything else that comes to mind. This doesn't all have to be done in one sitting. You may want to start and stop, read and revise. Whatever your process looks like is fine, just get it all on paper. When you feel like you've said everything you need to say, read it aloud to a loved one or to your therapist so that someone bears witness to your hurt and then burn or shred it.

There is no timeline for how long this process should take. It takes as long as it takes for you to move through it and then let it go. If you are able to finish the letter but notice you feel hesitant to read it or let it go, write about that separately. What's coming up for you when you think about sharing it or letting it go? If you're working with a therapist, these are excellent things to process with them. Once you get to the place where you're ready to let it go, then do so. It doesn't mean that you won't ever think about this person again or that the pain will vanish; this process is helpful in symbolically giving yourself permission to move forward.

Enlist the Help of a Reporter

The process of notifying others after a friendship has ended can be grueling, especially if there are lots of mutual friends or family involved. Enlist the help of one friend who can act as a reporter to tell the others what has happened. This person should be equipped with only the details you would like to be shared and can act as a conduit for all those perhaps well-meaning but exhausting inquiries. The reporter can let others know that you're not interested in going into any further details and can answer any questions others may have about what you may need at this time. This will also help to avoid any speculation or having to constantly rehash whatever events led to the breakup in the first place. Anybody who is grieving doesn't want to have to keep repeating the story and reopening those wounds. It's important to remember that when we're hurting, the people who love us typically want to be helpful. Allowing someone to serve in this role gives them guidance about how to do so.

Talk with Someone Who Gets it

Because the grief that comes with a friendship ending is often invalidated, it's important to talk about how you're feeling with someone who will not downplay your feelings. Someone who won't tell you that "you have plenty of other friends so there's no need to be sad." After this type of loss, it's important to confide in someone who will honor your grief and help you hold it. This is when talking with a therapist or a support group of others who have experienced a similar loss can be helpful. In writing this book, I spoke with so many sisters who have experienced a comparable pain and the overwhelming response is that sharing our stories with others who really get it typically helps us to feel less alone.

Put Together a Coping Kit

Grief often happens in waves. It rises and then falls. Unfortunately, many of us will typically avoid allowing ourselves to experience the fullness of our grief for fear of being swallowed by it. Putting together a kit of items that help you to ride the waves can be a great way to take care of your future self. You want to start by beautifully decorating a box you already own or purchasing a new decorative box and then including in it a book that you can get lost in, word games or a puzzle to put together, a journal and pen, your favorite scented lotion or a candle, something that is tactile like Play-Doh, a stress ball or a fuzzy piece of fabric, an index card filled with affirmations that remind you of who you are and that this moment will pass, a favorite treat (perhaps some sour candy, Life Savers, or something else you can chew on), and a favorite meditation or breathing exercise that typically calms you. Now this list is pretty long and as you might imagine, if you wait until you are too overwhelmed to begin collecting these items, it will likely only increase your overwhelm.

The key is to get these items together when the tide has gone out, putting them in the box where they will be easily accessible when those waves come crashing in.

MAKE SOME PLAYLISTS TO MATCH YOUR MOODS

As we discussed earlier, the dual process model for non-death losses and grief suggests that we move in and out of thoughts and feelings that help us either focus on the loss or rebuild our lives after the loss. There is no hierarchy. Both are needed. One of the most powerful ways I have found to help navigate my emotions is through music. Making a playlist that matches both sides of our grieving process can be very helpful in assisting us in honoring what we're feeling during any given time. Make one playlist full of songs, poems, etc., that help you to embrace feelings of sadness, anger, and disappointment, and make another full of tracks that leave you feeling hopeful, joyful, and optimistic. Again, there is no right or wrong, only what you need in the moment.

GO SIT DOWN SOMEWHERE

This is one of those phrases I heard my grandmother repeat so often that I can still hear it as clear as day in her voice: "Go sit down somewhere." Now when I heard this as a little girl, it was typically because I was trying to sit on the porch and be in grown folks' business or was bopping around after having been told to stop several times. But as an adult, I hear it as a loving invitation to stop and attend to something. We all have our ways of avoiding thoughts and feelings that feel too big. We shop, drink, work, find a new boo, take on a new hobby, etc. But there is no outrunning, outworking, or outshopping grief. It demands to be honored and the sooner we clear space to do so, the better off we are. Allow yourself to cry and cuss. Allow yourself to mope and lie around. Allow yourself to tend to yourself and the parts of you that are aching. It is okay to admit that you are in pain and that a hurtful thing has happened. It hurts because it was important, and good-byes are hard. Work hard against shaming yourself or allowing others to shame you for the sadness related to having to say good-bye to someone who was important to you. Take the time and space you need to care for you.

BUT THEY ARE STILL *THERE!*

A big challenge with the ending of a friendship occurs when we still have to see the person we're no longer friends with. Maybe it was your work bestie who always shared lunch—and tea—with you and now lunchtime feels awkward and uncomfortable. Or maybe it's a longtime friend who is still close to members of your family, or you share a significant number of mutual friends. In either instance, managing those scenarios is part of the grieving process.

The easiest approach is to change your routine. Is it possible to go to lunch an hour earlier or later? Maybe you press pause on face-to-face church service and attend virtually for a while so that you can give both of you space. There is nothing wrong with taking some time to avoid a confrontation or an encounter with the person—especially if your emotions are running high. And, yes, it's entirely possible that making these accommodations in the short term may activate some old hurts from earlier in your life. Anytime there is a present rejection, it's possible that the memory of a past rejection will be triggered, along with the emotions that came with it. This is another reason why changing your routine might be the best course of action for you in the short term. Doing so might also free up some time for you to do the inner work necessary to heal your hurt over the lost friendship and make space for new friends, which I will talk about in part IV.

I wish I could tell you that your friendship breakups will fall neatly into one of the three categories discussed earlier in this chapter: a life change, physical/emotional distance, or betrayal. Unfortunately, that's not always how it works. Some relationships just end and there isn't a reason. In those cases, it can be hard to embrace a loss where we can't definitely say "Oh, she did this!" or "We don't talk anymore because of this." But the truth is that people's interests shift. We grow, we change, and sometimes stuff just isn't a fit anymore. It doesn't have to mean that she was bad, that you were bad, or that a bad thing happened. It just means things are different. And even when we don't like it or agree with it, it's important to know that it's okay.

QUESTIONS FOR REFLECTION

1. What signs do you think indicate that a friendship is over? If you've had the experience of ending a friendship, what let you know that it was over?

2. What does it look like to have closure after the end of a friendship? Are there certain rituals or practices you've engaged in to mark the end of a relationship?

3. If a friend wanted to end their relationship with you, would you want them to tell you about it or just stop answering your calls? Do you think there are pros and cons for each approach? What are they?

CHAPTER 10

Sisterhood Is Most Needed in the Places You Wouldn't Expect It

No matter what accomplishments you make,
somebody helped you.

–Althea Gibson

It may be easier to see sisterhood in action when we're talking about our more intimate relationships, but as I noted briefly earlier, it's also important for us to recognize what sisterhood looks like in a more global sense and get clear about what it means to move in the spirit of sisterhood in our interactions with Black women we may not know. Of course, one version of sisterhood looks like being there to wipe your girl's tears after she has gone through a bad breakup, or to cheer in the stands as she walks across the stage to receive her master's degree. But sisterhood is much more expansive than that. What does sisterhood look like as we think about our business practices? What does sisterhood look like in advocacy work? What does it look like in the academy? What does it look like in any space we occupy? It's common to hear the refrain "It's not personal, it's just business," but I'd argue that it's always personal when we're dealing with another sister.

Much of my work and my life, quite frankly, is guided by a simple statement: I trust the goodness of Black women. Because I trust this, I am confident that the world would and could look much differently if more of us believed and acted in this way. Author and podcaster Laura Cathcart Robbins recently shared a video of herself telling a story from her childhood about flying as an unaccompanied minor. Before she walked off with the white flight attendant who would be accompanying her on the flight, her father instructed her that if anything happened while on the plane to "look for a sister." She knew what he meant. He meant to look for a Black woman. She went on to talk about how years later she holds on to his advice and finds herself scanning a room, any room, to see whether there are sisters present. If there aren't, she "looks for the exits." Laura understands the assignment. She understands the essence of global sisterhood.

SIS GOT US OUT HERE LOOKING MESSY

I get the importance of being a "good" sister within my personal circle of friends, but it's harder when I see sisters I don't know not doing right by us. You know that saying "We all we got"? Well, some of us don't got us at all. It's hard enough dealing with the oppressive systems out here, but when it's our own, I feel really sad. I guess it's true that all skinfolk ain't kinfolk. There are some Black women with large platforms who are scamming their sisters or simply not representing sisterhood at all, and I have no idea what I can do to "pull their coattails," as my granny used to say. Or even if I should.

—*Marcia, 58*

What Marcia is talking about here is one of those topics that needs to be discussed at the next secret Black girl meeting. You know those topics you talk about in the group chat but not typically in public because every conversation ain't for everybody? This is one of them. So let's just pretend it's only me, you, and a few thousand of your closest girlfriends chatting for a second.

A 2021 study on group processes and intergroup relations actually explains what Marcia might be feeling:

Of interest in the present study is the role of collective threat, or the concern that the poor behavior of an ingroup member will be generalized into negative judgments about the whole group . . . Social identity theorists argue that people use their social identities as a point of self-definition and evaluation, and thus are motivated to maintain a positive image of their own social group . . . When negative stereotypes against one's group are confirmed, ingroup members are likely to feel threatened because these reinforce negative perceptions of their group . . . This threat can, in turn, increase hostility toward those ingroup members who appear to perpetuate the negative stereotypes.[1]

So Marcia's frustration at Black women whom she perceives as "scammers" is possibly centered on how their behavior will reflect on Black women as a collective, causing more than just the immediate harm of lost money or poor service. For those of us for whom sisterhood is a value, it is often hard to see other Black women co-opt the language and loyalty of sisterhood without actually operating in sisterhood as a practice. When we got us, it's glorious. When we don't, it's often painful. We'll discuss both sides of the spectrum here.

SISTERHOOD IN THE ACADEMY

During the summer of 2021, one of the biggest stories, at least among Black women, was the utterly ridiculous debacle related to Professor Nikole Hannah-Jones, a Pulitzer Prize–winning journalist and the creator of the 1619 Project, a collection of writing that reframes American history by placing "slavery and its continuing legacy at the center of our national narrative,"[2] being denied a tenured position at her alma mater, the University of North Carolina at Chapel Hill. This was a particularly activating experience for many Black women because it was a classic example of how you can work to be the best at what you do and still be denied what others receive with far fewer credentials or brilliance. Many Black women expressed concern over how Professor Hannah-Jones was treated and did what was possible to show support. One sister, Dr. Lisa Jones, an associate professor of pharmaceutical sciences at the University of Maryland, Baltimore, withdrew her name from consideration for a faculty position in the Chemistry Department at UNC-Chapel Hill in a show of solidarity with Professor Hannah-Jones. In a written statement, Dr. Jones affirmed, "While I have never met Ms. Hannah-Jones, as a faculty member of color, I stand in solidarity with her and could not in good conscience accept a position at UNC."[3]

After hearing about Dr. Jones's withdrawal, Professor Hannah-Jones shared the following via Twitter: "I've never met this sister, Dr. Lisa Jones, but the solidarity shown me by Black women in particular during this crucible is something I will never forget." Reports indicated that Dr. Jones had been being recruited by the UNC Chemistry Department for two years before withdrawing her application. This position may have been a game changer for her and her career, but after seeing the way Professor Hannah-Jones was treated, she quickly realized that the cost may have been too great. Yes, she could have sucked it up as we often do in the interest of our careers, but she seems to have recognized the importance of sisterhood in practice.

I can acknowledge that this was a huge risk for Dr. Jones, and it's not one that can be made in every circumstance, but certainly the spirit of the decision she made can be considered should we find ourselves in similar situations. Let's also not miss the appearance of a balm expressed in the tweet from Professor Hannah-Jones. I can only imagine the anger, hurt, disappointment, and range of other emotions she experienced as she navigated that experience. I am sure that knowing she did not have to carry all of that alone offered at least a little comfort. You might be thinking, *Well, of course Black women stood behind her and supported her.* It is our customary and expected behavior in a situation like this. But this is precisely why that instinct to stand in solidarity with one another must be protected. We've not seen the last experience like this. The systems will unfortunately continue doing what they do against us. There will be many more times when we will need to rally to support a sister.

That support can show up in a myriad of ways. Maybe it means supporting a sister through the seemingly daily microaggressions that arise while working in the primarily white spaces that dominate academia. If there are no or very few Black advisers or administrators on your particular campus, what can you do to advocate in that space? If you're a sister who has been through the hurdles of the dissertation process, can you give pointers to another sister who might be struggling? Not just with her work—she might have that on lock. But how did you balance the workload? How did you implement self-care throughout the process? Or maybe you didn't and you want to warn her to not make the same mistakes you did. I love what Tia Sherèe Gaynor wrote in her "Love Letter to Black Women in the Academy," an essay in *Inside Higher Ed:* "The armor you wear may reduce the impact of the scars left from all the large and tiny cuts inflicted upon your minds, bodies and spirits but is heavy to carry . . . We have many ways to heal ourselves from the harms inflicted upon us as we navigate the halls of predominantly white institutions. Some people, like me, build community in sister circles."[4] What a moving and brilliant way to encourage and affirm sisters who are navigating the land mines of academia.

Yes, Sis. This is all labor, I know. Sometimes we want the privilege of just showing up, being our excellent selves in the classroom and in our chosen committees and programs, and then going home to our safe spaces. But maybe, just maybe, if we find ways to support one another, we can make these public spaces safer as well. At the end of the day, the fuel that allows this engine to continue is reciprocity—remember that? It is each of us doing our part to see and be of service to one another that gives us the bandwidth to jump into action when needed.

———

SISTERHOOD IN BUSINESS

As noted previously, the way that Black women rally around one another in situations where other Black women have been wronged is a large part of what sisterhood looks like in action. It is one of the things I love most about us, and it is also one of the things that gets easily exploited, which is painful to watch. An incident of sabotage aimed at a sister-owned business during the spring of 2022 gave us an opportunity to see in real time the various phases Black women can go through in an effort to put sisterhood into action. Here's what happened:

Honey Pot, a Black woman–owned, feminine hygiene products company, came under fire after making changes to the formula of its Honey Pot Foaming Wash. Sisters had rallied around Honey Pot for years and were not only the earliest adopters of the products but also some of its fiercest supporters. In 2020, the owner of Honey Pot, Beatrice "Bea" Dixon, appeared in national commercials for Target to talk about her products and how having them on shelves in Target had positively impacted her business. Well, the racists of the world did not like that a Black woman and her products were being heralded in this way by Target and began leaving one-star reviews on Target's website. Enter a whole fleet of Supa Sistas. We did what we always do to right a wrong. Black women flooded the site with positive reviews and emptied the shelves to show support. So, when a video was shared in the spring of 2022 comparing an old bottle of the wash with the new one, the hairs on the backs of the necks of faithful users, overwhelmingly sisters, stood up. It was an all too familiar feeling, that sinking in the pit of your stomach that signals something isn't right, and while you don't know exactly what's about to happen, it doesn't feel good. On the surface, there were concerns about negative physical reactions to the new ingredients, curiosity about why there had not been more transparency, and rumors that the brand had been sold and was no longer actually Black owned.

The proverbial sirens wailed.

While concerns around formula changes, especially as they relate to products for the vagina, are to be taken seriously, what appeared to be simmering underneath these concerns was a feeling of seeming betrayal. How could this brand that we, as Black women, supported from the beginning turn its back on us not only with a new formula, but perhaps with a new non-Black owner? It was a story we'd read and lived so many times before. When products that are initially built with Black women in mind are then sold and no longer meet our needs, changes are often made that prioritize profit over care. We often find ourselves feeling like these brands are built on the backs of our support only for us to be discarded when new management insists they be something that "everyone" can enjoy. We ask: "Why can't we ever have anything that is just ours?" And what do we do when an old scar is scratched to reveal a now fresh wound?

Let's dig deeper here because this is way more nuanced than we generally admit. There is often a deep pain that we are not always skilled or gentle at managing when these perceived betrayals happen. The white supremacist systems in place make us necessarily hypervigilant when it comes to "our" things and thrive when we point the finger at one another—in this case the owner of the company, Beatrice—instead of where it belongs. And instead of asking for help in dressing the wound created by the situation or sharing our fears around what this new wound might mean or sitting still long enough to allow the wound to heal just a little, we barge forward trying to take care of it the best way we know how, even if that means that our sisters on either side of the issue are injured. That initial hair standing up on the back of our neck and sinking feeling in the pit of our stomach then becomes an all-out battle that we are determined to survive by any means necessary.

Within a matter of hours, there was post after post of sisters sharing how sad and angry they were about these changes. There were harsh posts calling Beatrice a sellout, and even reportedly threatening her. These attacks are not okay and not how we should strive to be in community with one another. But I do understand how we got there.

A few days into the uproar, Beatrice released a heartfelt and at times tearful video explaining the changes that had been made to the formula, largely to improve it and make it safer to use, and make it clear that she and her brother still own the company. She asked for grace and patience as she continued to learn about running a business at this scale and invited customers to keep asking her questions via email. She showed up in far more grace than had been extended to her and reframed the feedback that had been shared throughout the weekend as clear love and support for the products. She got it. She seemed to understand what was activated for sisters with the news and wanted to do what she could to heal the fresh wound. If I were to take it a step further, I would suggest we all look at the real enemy, the systems that thrive off our scarcity mindsets. There are so many valuable conversations to be had relating how we move forward with one another.

First, it's very important for us to recognize when our feelings are bigger than the situation calls for and to learn how to manage them. In the Honey Pot example, feeling disappointed and sad that one of your favorite products no longer has the same formula is a proportional response to the situation. Wishing ill on or threatening the founder of the company because of changes to the product is disproportionate to what has happened. Anytime we find ourselves having a reaction that is disproportionate to the original event, it is a sign that something deeper is at work. We are likely dealing with a case of a fresh wound being formed where there was an old scar. In this instance, the best thing to do is to take a step back, give ourselves some time and distance from the activating event, and then get curious about what has happened for us in the moment. Asking ourselves questions about whether we have felt a similar feeling before and exploring the story we've created about what's happening can help us all get closer to what really needs to be tended to. In this case, perhaps it was a sense of feeling betrayed or discarded, so to speak.

Second, and likely a question that many people may not expect to see associated with sisterhood, is what responsibility do Black women business owners have to Black women when their products are targeted to us? Are there any? I mean, nobody likes to feel like they have been used or as if they were a placeholder until white dollars arrive, but is that not the capitalist structure so many of us have bought into? The goal for most businesses, at least under this framework, is to try to make as much money from as many people as possible. How do we wrestle with the idea that there is a different standard of responsibility for business owners who target Black women? Is there one? I think there is when a Black woman is at the helm of said business. Maybe part of the work of being a leader in this capacity is to show the ultimate demonstration of sisterhood based on the way you treat the customer who looks like you. So how might a Black woman business owner or organizational leader reimagine what business looks like so that the end goal is not always making the most money? To somehow weave those 4 Ss of Sisterhood that I proposed earlier in the book throughout the mission of the business or organization? Given the ways that Black women show up to support those who support them, I think it's entirely possible. A good place for all of us to start is for businesses and organizations to be as transparent as possible in their communications with the Black women they target, and for Black women to rethink what we believe about our own power in these spaces.

As a collective, both Black women business owners and those of us who support them must examine the power of our mobilization. When we demand change or want notice, there is no doubt that as a global sisterhood we can get it. It was Black women who started #BlackLivesMatter and birthed a movement. It was a Black woman who started #SayHerName and drove attention to the Black women who were also being disproportionately harmed by police. It was a Black woman who began the work of #MeToo in support of sexual assault survivors. The ability to mobilize our collective voice is a wonderful thing for a business or a brand or another entity when it's working in their favor. It can be devastating when it's not. The hard truth is that the internet and social media have sometimes made us move in a way, particularly with our sisters, that we would not face-to-face. I seriously doubt any sister would actually threaten Beatrice to her face. Yes, under the belief she'd sold the company to white owners, I know there's some firecracker out there who'd whisper (or not) "sellout" under her breath. But the decorum we practice in our "real" lives should not disappear just because we are behind a screen. I'll dig into that more later.

The point is, it's going to be absolutely critical for a Black business that targets Black women to be willing to unpack a few things if it decides to make a shift. First, why? What's driving the change? Yes, get your bag, Sis. But also know what that bag is going to cost not just you but your sisters too. And if you are the Black woman being targeted, think about how you might respectfully air your frustrations in a way that's not harmful. I think what both sides will find is that when sisterhood is the underlying motivation, there is room for more grace *and* strategy.

SISTERHOOD IN INDUSTRY

I'll never forget the morning I awakened to multiple threads in my social media newsfeeds capturing the sisterhood of journalists and other media contributors. Apparently, some of my favorite Black women in media had taken a trip to the Caribbean islands for some much-needed R&R. Before seeing pictures from this trip, I figured that they all had collegial relationships with one another, but after seeing the pictures it was clear that this was not just a vacation with colleagues. It was a for real sister circle. I was simultaneously ecstatic that they were able to curate this experience for themselves and devastated that, because of the pandemic, my nerves were too bad for me to gather with my girls. I craved that desperately. The photos were beautiful, including their golden black and bronze skins, jewel-toned caftans, and matching Telfar bags. But more than anything, it was the captions that hit me like a ton of bricks. Each one of them expressed just how much they needed that time away. After more than eighteen months of a pandemic, continued racial unrest, and bout after bout of grief and loss, their hearts, minds, and bodies longed for the kind of healing that could have only come from that getaway.

Fast-forward to months and years later, I imagine that a part of what was forged during that trip has sustained many of them through public criticism, doxing attempts, and career transitions. Notably, when Tiffany Cross was unceremoniously dismissed from MSNBC in November 2022, it was this same sister circle who publicly and privately rallied around her with an abundance of support. Joy-Ann Reid used a portion of her show, also on MSNBC, the evening Tiffany was dismissed to share a loving and pointed message of support: "She's not just my friend, she is my sister. . . . You don't understand how sisters move. . . . Her sisters will be here to support anything Tiffany Cross ever does." If you think back to the conversations we had in chapter 6 about how systems, like mainstream media, often pit Black women against one another, you understand what it means for Joy-Ann to make this kind of statement on the very same network that had dismissed Tiffany. You understand why Joy-Ann made it.

The sisterhood forged by these women is, of course, unique to them, but it is emblematic of what Black women create anytime we find ourselves in a space in which we are not the majority. We understand that our success both individually and collectively depends on support from one another and so where none exists, we create it. In virtually any field you can think of, Black women have created a support network so that when sisters enter, they are not alone and are supported on their journeys. There are associations and organizations for Black women attorneys, photographers, soccer players, makeup artists, etc. Even when more formal organizations don't exist, these networks of support and mentorship still do. In chapter 6, when I discussed the role Ms. Joyce had in helping me transition into my role at CAU, that network was at play. When you see a table full of sisters at a lunch spot, it is very likely that this group is functioning in a similar way. In your own life, I imagine that you have been part of a network like this, or perhaps you were drawn to this book because you're longing for something like this.

When asked about the importance of having a Black woman mentor as a doctoral student, one participant in a study published in 2018 stated, "It is easier for me to open up to someone who resembles me. I feel that an African American woman can better understand my struggles in academia, society, and life overall because she has probably experienced the same struggles herself."[5] I think this is what many of us are looking for, people who intimately understand the ins and outs of not only our industry but also our lived experiences. Someone who can help us make sense of what we might be experiencing and offer strategies on how to move forward. Because large-scale disparities still exist in terms of Black women climbing the ranks in many fields, these informal networks are often critical for success.

SISTERHOOD IS NOT FOR SALE

Researchers have found that consumers have more positive attitudes toward and a stronger intention to buy products when they have been endorsed by celebrities with whom consumers have built a parasocial relationship.[6] Parasocial relationships refer to nonreciprocal relationships that fans or consumers develop as a result of repeated media consumption.[7] Since our favorite online influencers and media personalities function in similar ways as celebrities in our worlds, it is more likely that when they suggest a product or service, we will try it. Think about some of your favorite Black women to follow online. How often have you bought something because they suggested it? I have all manner of skincare products, clothing, and accessories in my closet and drawers all because some fly sister introduced them to me. When I think about the Black women who most often influence my purchases, they do feel like people I am in community with. I know information about the cities they live in, the things they enjoy, even some of their fears if they've shared them. I don't claim to "know" them, but there is a sense of familiarity because of the information they willingly share about themselves online. There is no doubt then that there are Black women who have figured out that this is an incredibly lucrative strategy, especially as it relates to Black women, because we often exercise our buying power to invest in products and services that make our lives easier, more enjoyable, and more beautiful.

Black women's tastes and purchases tend to influence the larger culture, and we are typically very loyal to the brands we love. In the beauty industry alone, Black women spend approximately $7.5 billion annually. So the potential to sell things to Black women, particularly if you create community with Black women, is high. And I'm here for all of that when the community-building and engagement are genuine. However, I am concerned when I see what appears to be performative sisterhood: a contrived sense of community from sisters online whose sole goal is monetary gain. It is not okay to sell the appearance of intimacy and closeness with other Black women when there is a new endeavor to promote, but Black women are absent from your inner circle. It is not okay to exploit the tendency many sisters have to "root for everybody Black" if your intention is not to bring as many sisters with you as possible. It is not okay to exploit the pain and longing to belong that so many sisters harbor by offering events and experiences that tout inclusion and affirmation only for them to leave feeling excluded and dejected.

Melanie, a forty-year-old sister in the TBG community, shared that she followed a popular career coach online who marketed her services to Black women. Melanie often found her advice helpful and thought that working with her through a small group coaching program she was offering might be a good idea, as she was planning for an eventual career change. Melanie shared that she reached out via email with several questions about the program before making the commitment and was taken aback by both the tone and content of the response she received from the career coach. She felt berated and belittled by the response, only to then see the coach share a de-identified copy of her email with her online followers as an example of someone who was not ready to invest in their future. This left Melanie feeling further "belittled, mocked, and frankly disappointed."

Perhaps this is a great opportunity for us to pause and integrate some of the things we've discussed so far in the book. Based on

Melanie's statement above, share your thoughts on the following questions:

1. What concerns you about the career coach's behavior?

2. How might the career coach have handled this situation differently?

3. What suggestions would you give Melanie for handling this situation?

4. Are there any systems from chapter 6 that might be impacting this experience?

Again, I realize that the challenge here is that many sisters might not see this as related to sisterhood at all. They view this as an isolated incident with one woman that has no real impact. However, the foundational premise of this idea of a global sisterhood is based largely in practicing what bell hooks refers to as a love ethic. She states that "embracing a love ethic means that we utilize all the dimensions of love—'care, commitment, trust, responsibility, respect, and knowledge'—in our everyday lives."[8] Being able to embody and utilize these dimensions in our relationships with our sisters gets us closer to creating the world we'd like to see.

SISTERHOOD AND ACCOUNTABILITY

Because we're human and not robots, we know that mistakes will happen. It is inevitable that the Black women we admire, shop with, and read about will make mistakes. So how do we, as a community of Black women, engage when we're disappointed, hurt, or angry? The first step is to remind ourselves of our humanity. We know that grace is often not given to us, so approaching any type of disappointment starting here is preferable. Next, it's important for us to be mindful about what we share in public spaces. Instead of going live on Instagram to express displeasure about an experience, an email or a direct message may be a better way to attempt to get clarity or share concerns. Now I want to be clear here that I am not talking about being silent as a way to cover for bad behavior because that is not helpful. What I am saying is that starting with more private communication is usually a more effective and compassionate strategy. And finally, I think we must be open to feedback from one another. In many ways, it feels like everything we've discussed prior to this point is what will allow us to get to this place. When we are connecting with one another with a spirit of care, it is easier to hear and offer feedback, even when it's difficult.

QUESTIONS FOR REFLECTION

1. Given what you know about how Black women relate to one another, what changes might we be able to see if a spirit of sisterhood was brought to situations where it's currently absent?

2. How might the ethos of sisterhood change our political landscape?

3. What changes might we see in our neighborhoods, schools, and places of worship if there was more intentional sisterhood?

4. What we've covered here are just a few examples, but what if we dared ourselves and one another to make our definition of sisterhood even more expansive?

PART IV

Following, Finding, and Fellowship

Life is short, and it's up to you to make it sweet.

–Sarah "Sadie" Delany

CHAPTER 11

The Complexities and Possibilities of Digital Sisterhood

The greatness of a community is most accurately measured
by the compassionate actions of its members.

—Coretta Scott King

In 1997, when I should have been writing essays for my English class or getting rest so that I could be ready for my Abnormal Psychology class, I vividly remember staying up until all hours of the night chatting in AOL and Yahoo! chat rooms. I was absolutely fascinated by the idea of connecting with people from all around the world, and my love for online spaces has only become more clear as I've been able to use them to create opportunities for Black women across the globe to connect with and support one another. I know that not everyone is a fan of the internet, so I fully own my bias here, but I do believe that online spaces remain one of the most powerful ways to meet sisters with whom we have lots in common. Furthermore, I think that technology has been an incredible conduit for capturing and cataloging the everyday experiences of Black women so that we feel even less isolated in our own lives. For instance, I wouldn't even have been aware of any of the examples of sisterhood I shared in chapter 10 if it were not for these women and others digitally sharing their experiences.

That said, online spaces aren't just excellent ways to share our stories. They also provide us with digital venues to heighten our experiences of being Black women. A great example of this was in the early months of quarantine and isolation during the Covid-19 pandemic, when the social media platform Instagram started seeing a boost in the use of its Instagram Live feature. Hip-hop producers and entrepreneurs Timbaland and Swizz Beatz were two of the first to capitalize on the apt attention of Black audiences by featuring soft battles between music producers and artists. They called it Verzuz, and at its high point, hundreds of thousands of people would gather in a virtual "room" and listen to their faves play their most popular hits.

For me and many other sisters, the Verzuz celebration featuring Jill Scott vs. Erykah Badu or Gladys Knight vs. Patti LaBelle felt like those familiar kitchen table, front porch, and salon spaces, only reinvented. We cackled at the light, harmless shade the artists would throw at each other, commented to one another about our favorite song or the spicy memory attached to it, and talked about the event to our real-life girlfriends for weeks afterward. At a time when we were parched for novel experiences and things to look forward to, those few hours in front of the computer screen spent imbibing the nostalgic music and genuine, love-filled conversations between those women offered a little bit of healing. In session 211 of the *Therapy for Black Girls* podcast, I spoke with Jennifer Sterling, a registered dance and movement therapist, about why things like the Verzuz battles were so special in that moment. She shared that the community we experienced during that time helped us to feel supported and less alone. In many ways, she explained, the experience of being together, even virtually, all hearing the same songs, allowed us to coregulate with the sound of the music and the voices we were hearing, which helps to soothe our nervous system.

STILL TRYING TO FIGURE IT OUT

I've been trying to connect with other Black women online for a while now. In some cases, it's gone great. I'm totally into planners and scrapbooking and I found a group on Facebook full of Black women who are into the same thing.

I think my biggest issue is figuring out how to move those relationships from being very light engagements over a shared interest to something deeper. I don't want to be the weirdo inviting everyone out for coffee a month after meeting them. I'd side-eye a sister if she did that to me. But I also want to connect more with a few of the women I met.

—Emma, 37

This is often the dilemma, isn't it? You meet someone and think they're cool but have no idea how to take things to the next level. Navigating relationships online can be challenging, especially if you have the expectation of wanting them to grow into something more. But it's not the desire for more that's the issue, nor is it the fact that, so far, your connections have remained pretty surface level. The issue might be the types of groups you are joining. I would suspect that someone who is joining a Facebook group for planners (or crocheting, exercise, reality TV, etc.) might not necessarily be looking for a best friend. At least not consciously. Maybe consider joining a group where the intention is for people to meet, to share their stories and hearts in a way that could lead to a deeper connection. This was actually one of the reasons why I started Three for Thursday. I'll talk more in depth about that in a minute.

How We Got Here

The earliest days of digital sisterhood can be traced back to the AOL chat lines of the mid- to late nineties. Following those more rudimentary formats for talking individually to new people, the world of digital sisterhood expanded to early social media platforms like BlackPlanet (1999) and Myspace (2003) and then ultimately to the comments sections of some of our favorite blogs and message boards: Sisterfriends (founded in 2001, now defunct), Very Smart Brothas (2008), and MyBrownBaby (2008). These comments sections would be the places where we could gather and weigh in on whatever the topic was but also catch up with some of our favorite commenters. We'd notice if a "regular" hadn't posted in a while and might even express concern, asking around to see if anyone had heard from them. In many ways, these spaces served as an early iteration of Black Twitter before Twitter existed.

I've spoken with a number of people who used sites like Sister-friends as a way to meet other like-minded Black women, especially when new to an area. "I have sisters who are still friends to this day from that site," said forty-five-year-old Michelle. "We're not as close as in those early days when we'd chat about any number of subjects and then schedule meetups to continue the conversation in person. And while we aren't as close today, we still keep in touch." I firmly believe that these sites and message boards walked so that social media platforms like Facebook, Instagram, and Twitter could run—and Snapchat and TikTok could fly. The ability to engage with people from around the world was enticing and expanded into what we now classify as social media.

From there, the formation of groups and communities housed within these platforms opened up even more opportunities for engagement. Facebook groups like Black Girls Garden and Black Girls Craft create a space where sisters can gather, chat, share ideas, laugh via meme or emoji, and connect in ways that might be challenging otherwise. People often start sharing their personal journeys and heartaches within these groups and, in many cases, are surrounded by some version of love and care, even if for a moment.

Black Twitter functions in a similar way, though not as concretely because there is no one place where Black Twitter is housed. There are different subsets of people having varying conversations, but it is most easily found on the days of big cultural moments. The day Beyoncé released her maternity photo announcing her pregnancy with the twins, the tweets were on fire. Every holiday, there are thousands of #BlackatThanksgiving or #BlackatChristmas threads that bring so much joy, laughter, and sometimes very subtle critique or commentary. In my mind, it is the closest thing we have to the global "Black people meetings" that many of us joke about. We use it to gather digitally to grieve cultural icons, to share commentary about our favorite shows, and to discuss the issues important to us. Twitter was also instrumental in the Movement for Black Lives that started in large part after the deaths of Trayvon Martin and Michael Brown, Jr. For Black women in particular, I have seen Twitter be incredibly useful as a means of receiving and offering mutual aid and furthering conversations about what it means to be a Black woman in this world. I often talk about Twitter being my favorite platform to participate in, largely because it has introduced me to some of the most brilliant, talented, and kindhearted sisters in the world.

SHE DON'T KNOW ME LIKE THAT

But as with anything there are challenges and difficulties around engaging in the global digital sisterhood. The rules feel different. Do we call our sisters out publicly when we feel there's been an error, or do we hit them in their DMs? If we do think critiquing a sister is okay, what does that look like? Particularly when it comes to our higher-profile sisters, what is our responsibility as consumers of Black art and politics and other social issues to protect or temper our conversations when in "mixed" company? I know the prevailing thought for some is that the anonymity of the internet means that we can say and do what we want to online. That's deeply problematic when we consider what we are trying to build in our sisterhood. The truth is, the notion that we never know what people are struggling with applies online also. If a sister is going online just for a laugh or a moment of mental rest, but she ends up in a difficult conversation with another sister, that engagement will have the opposite effect. It doesn't hurt to think about that when we're interacting with people.

For all the good that can come from engaging with one another digitally, one of the difficulties that shows up is that it often feels as though we forget that there are real people on the other side of our screen. And in some ways, that's understandable. We exist online as screen names with a tiny avatar, not in the fullness of who we are and our experiences. Because Black women are often the ones most bullied and harassed in online spaces, it is important to be as tuned in to one another's humanity as possible. While there may be different rules of engagement for online behavior, I think our starting point should be how we would engage if we were interacting in real life. For example, I recently saw a post a sister shared online that was a picture of her kids' nursery. Someone commented, "I wouldn't have chosen that as artwork." What? Why exactly is that comment necessary? Let's stop and think about how something like this might play out in real life. Would you see a sister walking down the street in a beautiful black dress and some hot pink heels and stop her to say, "Black shoes would have gone better with that outfit"? Probably not. You might think it, but chances are you wouldn't go up to her and say it. Yet, this is how we interact online. It's so important to think about what might be driving our behavior to do these kinds of things "behind the screen" and consider the impact that hundreds if not thousands of comments like this might have on someone's mental health.

Additionally, it can be challenging to read one another well online. What you might consider to be a benign comment might not be read as such and therefore received as an insult. Which, of course, might cause someone who also doesn't interact well online to respond in kind. If we really think about it, every Twitter beef has come down to somebody saying something that somebody else didn't like, with the person on the receiving end not knowing how to communicate the fact that their feelings were hurt. So that person claps back and round and round we go.

I don't mean to suggest that our online relationships should function exactly like our real-life relationships. They are bound to be different. But the goal should always be to keep our digital spaces healthy and, in the best cases, spaces where people can grow and heal.

———

THE INTERNET IS NOT YOUR THERAPIST

I've also been thinking a lot about how we might be using digital spaces to get certain needs met, which inevitably ends with our disappointment because, frankly, the internet is not designed or formatted to meet needs in a way that is truly fulfilling or healing. Our needs for affirmation, validation, and praise are natural and human, but our chances of getting these needs met are far higher if we ask for them from people with whom we have existing relationships rather than strangers online. Even when we share something in what we believe to be the safety of our own followers, we never know where it will be reshared and reposted, and in essence, we might find ourselves inviting commentary that is by definition the opposite of the affirmation and validation we were seeking.

On the other hand, online communities can be incredibly powerful in offering a certain level of care and support, particularly for Black women, people with disabilities, the Black LGBTQIA community, people who live in rural areas, and those who may be slower to warm up in real life. You name it, and I have seen Black women support it—from new school clothes for someone's kids to lifesaving medical procedures and everything in between. Sisters may not be able to offer intimate or personalized feedback based on something that is shared in a digital space, but they often offer valuable guidance or direction: "Girl, this book helped me when I was dealing with that" or "Keep going, Sis. You're doing a good job." Black women, for the most part, move online in a way that says, "I got you, we gon' be alright."

At times, I find myself simultaneously awestruck and terrified about the vulnerability I see sisters displaying online, particularly younger sisters. I admire the ways they seem to be comfortable sharing some of the most painful and private parts of their lives but am terrified because the internet has shown time and time again that it is not a safe space for us. For many sisters who have grown up with social media always being present in their lives, I often wonder if sharing about a difficult situation on TikTok really is equivalent to me having a gabfest with my line sisters on the quad when I was their age. I also wonder how much of this sharing is prompted by feeling as though this is what needs to be posted to get noticed online as our attention spans vanish with warp speed. At the end of the day, I worry that this public vulnerability is replacing true intimacy that can actually hold, affirm, and challenge them when needed. I hope that in addition to the sharing that happens online they are also practicing what vulnerability looks like privately.

It seems that much of the online sharing and public vulnerability can best be understood through the context of parasocial relationships. It is why so many of us saw ourselves as an extension of the Huxtable family or considered ourselves the fifth friend in the sister circle of Issa, Molly, Tiffany, and Kelli. There is a sense of intimacy, perceived closeness (i.e., friend in my head), and identification that develops as a result of repeated media consumption. Until recently, TV characters, radio personalities, and celebrities were typically the objects of parasocial relationships, but with the advent of social media, video platforms like YouTube, and podcasting, individuals outside of these areas have become the objects as well. While in some ways parasocial relationships may foster a sense of community and sisterhood, they also allow for a certain type of exploitation that can threaten sisterhood.

RULES FOR DIGITAL ENGAGEMENT

As has been discussed, the potential power that our digital sisterhoods can wield is great. For some people, especially the disabled or those with social anxiety, the internet is one of the only opportunities available to make new connections. To that end, it may be helpful for us to have some "rules for engagement" in digital spaces. This list is not meant to be exhaustive, but more of a starting place to consider how we might go about building the digital world we'd like to inhabit with and for one another.

———

#1—*Celebrate Publicly and Criticize Privately*

Okay, so listen: We're going to need to talk through this one. I know it feels like there's something a little old school about this, but it still seems to have some value. Perhaps because I am a child of the "what goes on in this house, stays in this house" era I do think there are some things that should not be discussed with a wider audience. However, I am also fully aware that this type of mentality has been used to protect and hide bad behavior as well as to shield those within our families who harmed us from being held accountable. I am not at all advocating for this. Still, I do want us to consider when and how public critique is offered as it relates to other Black women.

I'm sure you've seen the pile-ons that often happen on social media. One person critiques a sister, then another, then another. The person might have already even said, "Yes. Okay. I got it. I know I did the wrong thing," but there are still fifteen more people who believe she shouldn't have done that thing and want to be sure that she knows they feel that way too. It can be too much for one person to hold. If you run across a wayward comment or post and you see that several other people have already commented on how wayward it is, perhaps consider just scrolling on. As I discussed earlier, because our online persona is often a flattened version of our existence, it can be easy to slip into engaging with others in ways that overlook and even dismiss their humanity. As much as possible, let's center that humanity when engaging with other sisters.

Another area that deserves some consideration is our engagement with popular media like TV and streaming series, books, movies, and music. Even while we have seen more projects with Black women at the helm in recent years, we know that the resources and opportunities given to sisters are not proportionate to the talent. That fact becomes complicated when many of us love nothing more than to gather with our Twitter timelines to talk about what we're watching, reading, and listening to. Perhaps, as it relates to projects by Black women, we should choose to be loud and ridiculous about the ones we love and only a little louder than a whisper about the ones we don't love so much. I think it's important to remember that everything ain't for everybody and that just because I don't love a thing does not mean a sister does not deserve the shot to make it.

Finally, we need to be conscious of public celebration and private critique when it comes to our engagement with Black women who are public figures, including politicians. Some level of public critique is fair for politicians to receive because they are elected officials and their job is to be responsible and accountable to their constituents. But we also know that Black women in these spaces are often targets for a kind of misogynoir that is relentless. Let's be mindful that we are critiquing policy, work, etc., but not the sister herself.

I know . . . there is definitely a flip side. Many of you might be reading this and saying, Shouldn't we engage our sisters online in the same ways we engage one another in real life? We don't hold back in the group dynamic. We're like "Sis, I love you, but you need to stop messing with him because he ain't doing you good." We don't hold back our critiques in those more intimate spaces, so, if we're going to say that digital sisterhood is this new extension of the old sisterhood format, or the way that we engage one another, then wouldn't those same rules apply? Yes, kind of. But we can't forget the fact that we're in mixed company. And in that mixed company, there are people who have the power to twist our words into something incredibly harmful for the Black woman receiving the critique. This should, in some way, at least factor into *how* we say what we say.

And the true difference is, if you're having that conversation with your girlfriend, there's an established relationship, so she automatically knows that you're coming from a place of love. Whereas if we're just blasting Young Black Sister TV Producer online, she doesn't know you from anybody. She doesn't know that it's coming from a place of love, nor should she assume that.

#2—Remember That You Don't Have to Comment on Everything

From a mental health standpoint, it's not healthy to feel like you have to weigh in on every single thing that happens in the world—regardless of whether it's your world, somebody else's world, or the world of Hollywood. There is a point where it gets to be too much, and we reach information overload. I'm not sure about you, but sometimes I will make a post or weigh in on a topic and then think, "Why did I even say that? I don't really care that much about this."

So, when you find yourself tempted to weigh in on what another sister has posted, ask yourself a couple of questions: (1) Has what I need to express already been shared by someone else? (2) What am I hoping to achieve by sharing what I plan to share? (3) Do I have a relationship with this person that would indicate they would even consider the points I have to offer or would change their mind? (4) Am I feeling some type of way about something else and using this opportunity to discharge that energy onto someone who has nothing to do with how I'm feeling? (5) Do I really care about this? If you feel satisfied with your responses to these questions, go ahead and post. If not, dig a little deeper to see what else in your interior world might need a little attention.

#3—Support Sisters Online

If you have it to spare, when you see sisters share their GoFundMe pages, Amazon wish lists, Cash App tags, etc., give if you can. If you don't have it to give, no worries. All of these avenues are simply modern-day iterations of the mutual aid we have been offering one another as a community for years. As I mentioned previously, I have seen sisters spring into action to support other sisters with a variety of needs, especially during the pandemic, when it became even more clear that we could not count on the systems in place to support or sustain us and our community. I know the concern around giving money is often "What if it's a scam?" and this is valid, but I also believe that when a gift is given, all that matters is your intention in giving it, not what happens next.

It's also important to note that supporting sisters online does not have to be monetary. You can also support sisters through your knowledge and expertise. Throughout the pandemic, when it seemed impossible to get clear and credible answers about how to navigate this new world with safety, I turned to those who I affectionately call "The Black Girl CDC." When I wanted information I could trust, I would scroll the Twitter timelines of Dr. Oni Blackstock, Dr. Uché Blackstock, Dr. Ebony Jade Hilton, Dr. Theresa Chapple, Dr. Kimberly Manning, and many other brilliant sisters who not only were on the front lines caring for patients during this crisis but also were making it a point to share their knowledge with the world via Twitter and other media. I have never met any of them, but they supported me and so many others through a very difficult time by simply sharing what they know. They serve as a powerful reminder for me that it is important to share our gifts and knowledge with the world because it is often of service to someone else.

DIGITAL SISTERHOOD IN ACTION

Now that we've discussed some of the benefits and difficulties of sisterhood in digital spaces, I want to share an example of what this digital sisterhood in action looks like at Therapy for Black Girls. As I've shared, Three for Thursday (TFT) began in early 2019 as a virtual town hall of sorts where I share three pieces of information, inspiration, or guidance to help members of the Therapy for Black Girls community get their lives together for the week. The gathering initially began on Facebook and Instagram Live but moved to Zoom for more privacy and logistical management. Sometimes members of the community send in suggestions for what they'd like to discuss and other times I choose topics based on what's happening in the news, pop culture, etc. On one particular Thursday I remember there were several heavy things on my heart to discuss, so I grabbed a quick lunch, gathered myself, and sat down at the computer to hold the space.

I opened the session with a talk about the difficulty we sometimes face as Black women in asking for what we need and want. I moved forward with unpacking my three points. Point #1: Somewhere early in life some of us were made to feel like we were wrong or too difficult when we asked for things. Point #2: Some of us may have bought into the fallacy that we're superwomen who don't need assistance. Point #3: Needing assistance has been weaponized against us, and some of us worry that asking for something means we owe somebody something.

"Oh, Dr. Joy preaching today!" one woman typed in the chat.

"Okay, let's pass the virtual collection plate," another woman unmuted herself and exclaimed.

"Why you gotta be so loud?!" came from another message in the chat.

Everyone in that Zoom room seemed to connect to these three points in such a powerful way. Based on their responses, the fear of asking for help resonated with them. I'd *seen* them, and they were clearly grateful. Following my sharing, the floor was opened for questions and/or comments related to the topic, praise reports, and other things sisters would like to share with the collective.

As you might imagine, this topic is something many sisters struggle with, so the conversation was filled with women sharing their experiences.

"I don't always feel worthy of asking for help."

"In the past, I've had people use my need for help against me. They throw it back in my face."

"It's hard to ask for help because it leaves me feeling exposed, naked. Open to harm."

Many women shared their painful experiences and explained why they often choose to go it alone. But there was also lots of sharing about instances where women did ask and actually got what they asked for. This is typical of our time together. Women taking the opportunity to be vulnerable in public, affirming one another, serving as possibility models for one another, and problem-solving. What happens when we gather on Thursday afternoons is not something I take lightly. One of the things I most enjoy about this space is the risks that sisters take in sharing what's going on with them. If this were a community where the expectation was that we'd be discussing crafts, we likely wouldn't see this level of transparency, but because they know the tone of the conversations and the kinds of topics we're likely to cover, it feels safe for them to share. Sure, if Three for Thursday was designed as a space where Black women came to get knitting tips, then what happened that day would have been completely inappropriate. And someone like Emma from earlier in this chapter might find herself feeling uncertain again about how to enrich, and potentially deepen, her encounters with the women in the group.

In any case, it is a high honor and responsibility that sisters know when I create a space, I will always do my best to keep it safe for them. What started out as a way for me to get a little closer to the members of our community has now turned into a weekly ritual that I love and that members love to participate in. This experience has taught me the power of online communities in enriching our sisterhoods.

Of the women-themed workshops and groups they ran in their center, psychotherapists and authors Luise Eichenbaum and Susie Orbach stated, "Twelve women sitting together focusing on a theme in their lives is a dramatic, tender, upsetting, and inspiring experience. Many workshops have a certain electricity, as the women painfully build together a psychological picture of their lives."[1] This is also an incredibly accurate description of Three for Thursday. When asked what she most enjoys about participating in TFT, Paula, age sixty-five, shared, "I enjoy the freedom that the format offers Black women to speak and share. Also, I love that I learn so much from the younger women and feel included vs. excluded. It's what Real Sisterhood looks like." Twenty-five-year-old Bianca commented that she enjoys "feeling part of the collective and discussing topics that I don't feel comfortable talking about with others."

Three for Thursday is a beautiful example of the way that technology has expanded our opportunities to meet one another and build relationships based on shared interests and goals. The internet, in its myriad iterations, has also allowed us to introduce the people in our real lives to one another in a way that feels magical. When we introduce our girlfriend at work who loves her Peloton as much as we do to the Black Girl Magic Peloton group on Facebook, we become a significant part of expanding one another's worlds. And maybe, just maybe, we help each other heal by the love, grace, and comradery that show up online.

QUESTIONS FOR REFLECTION

1. What rules guide your interactions with other Black women online?

2. Do you think digital spaces are able to foster vulnerability in a way that is helpful for all involved?

3. What other guidelines would you add to the list to help create healthy digital spaces for Black women to engage?

CHAPTER 12

Finding Your People

I'd rather regret the risks that didn't work out
than the chances I didn't take at all.

–*Simone Biles*

When we first started our time together, I shared many of the glorious benefits of developing and sustaining friendship with other sisters. Yes, there's plenty of research that shows how our physical and mental health is nourished by these relationships, but at the core of it all is that our sisterfriends tap into that part of us that longs for connection. In the face of whatever dehumanization or even inner struggles we might endure as Black women, that siren within us that goes off when we feel loved and cared for by a friend is a reminder, a proclamation even, of our humanity. Healthy friendships contribute to both our wellness and our wholeness.

I know Drake made it popular to proclaim "no new friends," but I have to strongly disagree with this sentiment. Being open to new sisterfriends at any stage of our lives should be a goal we all aim for. The truth is that you probably haven't met all the people who will love you, and being open to finding new people who can add to the rich relationships you might already have is a kind and loving act toward your own healing. I experienced the power of this myself recently.

Dr. Key, whom I mentioned earlier in the book, is my newest

close friend, and I met her in 2019 when we were both speakers at a conference in Atlanta. We both kind of knew of each other's work but had never actually met in person. When I saw and spoke to her at the Thursday night opening dinner, there was an instant connection, not unlike that immediate, love-at-first-sight romantic connection, but in our case platonic. She was just a bright light I was drawn to immediately and the feeling was mutual. When we came face-to-face, we grabbed each other up in a big hug and sparks flew.

Of course, we all know from our romantic relationships that sparks can fly in the beginning and later on we may find out that the person we had that instant connection with is not someone we want to spend time with. But gratefully, that wasn't the case for me and Dr. Key. After multiple conversations, we learned that we had many of the same values and seem to be wired similarly. She is from the South—her Mississippi to my Louisiana. We even later learned that we were both AKAs from different chapters. Interestingly, I don't think we thought we were going to be great friends when we met. Yes, there was a spark, but neither of us was necessarily looking for more friends. We talked professionally and connected with each other at other events, and the relationship organically grew. We stayed in contact, we bonded over the work we were doing, and we became close. She is definitely one of my people.

I JUST WANT TO FIND MY PEOPLE

Make new friends? Ugh, that has to be the hardest thing in the world for me to do. When I was little, all I had to do was show up in the same space with other kids and usually someone would come over to me and ask to play. But now that I'm grown, it doesn't happen like that. I've always been a shy person, so the idea that I have to actually go into a place and talk to people is terrifying. I know it's time for me to expand my friend group and to meet people who align with my current interests—I really want to find my people—

but it's just so challenging to build up the courage to put myself out there like that.

—*Tonia, 29*

Tonia, you are by far not alone. Finding friends as an adult is a whole different ballgame than when we were kids. While I wish for all of us as many serendipitous experiences with other sisters as we can stand, I am also well aware that connecting with new people whom you might eventually call friends is not typically so easy. There are many factors to consider. In session 118 of the *Therapy for Black Girls* podcast, psychologist and author Dr. Marisa G. Franco joined me as a guest to share some of the aspects to consider in making new friends. We began the conversation by talking about how easy it seemed to make new friends when we were in grade school and college and how it seemed much more difficult to do this as adults. She shared that the idea that making friends should be easy and doesn't require any effort is actually not setting us up for success and may be working against us. She went on to say that the reason why friendships seemed so easy in grade school and college was due to two things: continuous unplanned interactions and shared vulnerability. She further shared that one way to manufacture the kind of continuous unplanned interactions that can aid in the development of a friendship is to do something like taking an improv class, but you could also choose something like joining a kickball team. The key is for it to be an environment where the same people are likely to show up week after week, and you're able to have some type of engagement with them.

During our conversation I also had the chance to ask Dr. Franco about one of the biggest issues that gets in the way of us making new friends—fear of rejection. Oh, did I just hit a nerve there? Stay with me. We're gonna get through this. She said that the best way to deal with the fear that no one will like us is to assume that many people in fact do like us. She shared that we are notoriously bad at predicting our likability factor and that far more people will like us than we give ourselves credit for. She went on to say that what often ends up happening with this fear of rejection is that it impacts our behavior. So we go to a networking event hoping to connect with some cool people but then we get in our own heads about no one there liking us and we spend half the night looking down at our phones or not going up to people and introducing ourselves, which communicates to others that we are not interested. It is not that people don't like us—they don't know us well enough to not like us—it is that we came off as uninterested, so they didn't feel like there was an invitation to engage.

Zora Neale Hurston said, "Sometimes, I feel discriminated against, but it does not make me angry. It merely astonishes me. How can any deny themselves the pleasure of my company? It's beyond me." I absolutely love this! To me, it expresses what Dr. Franco was getting at. We too often think people dislike us more than they actually do. In general, we don't tend to judge that very well. But Sister Zora flips that on us. She speaks with confidence to anyone who will listen and essentially says, "Of course they like me. Why would they deny themselves the pleasure of my company?" Whew! I need a sip of water here. Anyone else?

In addition to the fear of rejection many of us may experience, it's important to address another issue that can make it difficult to find our people and that is social anxiety disorder (SAD). While many of us may be shy or a little awkward in social situations or wouldn't describe ourselves as the life of the party, these characteristics are not social anxiety disorder. SAD is a persistent and intense fear of being in social environments because we are afraid that we may be humiliated, criticized, or embarrassed. It can be hard to connect with new people if the idea of being in social situations is so distressing that you often avoid them.

In session 138 of the podcast, Janaya Sadler, a licensed clinical social worker in North Carolina who specializes in helping those who struggle with SAD, joined me to talk about treatment options. The first she discussed was cognitive behavioral therapy (CBT). A CBT approach would focus on the negative thoughts and limiting beliefs you may have as they relate to social situations. You may be asked to talk about the worst thing that can happen if you decide to engage socially. One of my favorite CBT exercises to use with clients is the "And Then What" (cue Young Jeezy) exercise. Let's say you were experiencing significant anxiety about a presentation you needed to give at work. The exercise might go like this:

> **ME:** *What's the worst thing that can happen if you stand up to give your presentation next month?*
>
> **YOU:** *I'll get up in front of the room and nothing will come out of my mouth.*
>
> **ME:** *And then what?*
>
> **YOU:** *Then everyone will just be staring at me, and I'll feel worse.*
>
> **ME:** *And then what?*
>
> **YOU:** *Then I'll look incompetent in front of my team.*

As you might imagine, this exercise can go on for some time but, as you continue to talk, I would be listening for the fear so that we can then discuss where the fear comes from and what resources you might need to assuage it. In another part of the exercise, I would ask you for evidence to support these thoughts.

Janaya also shared with the audience that social skills training is another treatment option for SAD. Because people who struggle with SAD often avoid social situations, the skills needed to interact are sometimes underdeveloped or rusty. She stated that she teaches clients effective communication, active listening, and conflict resolution so that they are better prepared to interact socially. Finally, Janaya discussed exposure therapy as a treatment for SAD. She mentioned that the purpose of exposure therapy is to reduce the anxiety and avoidance of the situation you are dreading. As part of exposure therapy, you work with your therapist to build a hierarchy of events starting with the least feared to the most feared and then you work through the hierarchy until the anxiety has lessened enough for you to approach the dreaded situation.

For example, let's say your college reunion is happening next summer and you really want to go and see old friends but are also consumed with anxiety about the idea of going because you're worried about what classmates who haven't seen you in ten years will say about you. You could start exposure therapy by looking through your college yearbook to refresh your memory about some of the classmates you might expect to see there. Next, you work up to joining one of the planning calls that has been organized for those who will be in attendance. Or perhaps you choose the outfit you plan to wear to the reunion; the steps would continue until you have reached the point where you are feeling ready to attend. The idea behind exposure therapy is that you are learning that you can tolerate the distress that occurs by getting closer to the thing that you fear.

A final barrier that often comes up when I am talking with Black women about finding their people is the idea that there is no place for them in the collective. For many, there appears to be a belief that there is only one way to be a Black woman and that if they do not fit this ideal, they do not belong. If you have not heard this from anyone else before, please hear me when I say there is a space for all of us who value being a part of the collective! Of course, we have different interests, different backgrounds, different personalities, but in my mind, these differences are assets. They have the potential to make all our experiences richer. Much of this stereotypical narrative is fed by what is seen in the media. If only certain kinds of stories are told about who we are as Black women, it is easy to see how someone might not believe they belong because they do not see themselves represented. This is why it is so important for each of us to share our stories in the ways that feel most comfortable to us. It is the only way that other sisters will know that they are not alone, that there is a place for them too.

THINK ABOUT FRIENDSHIP DIFFERENTLY

Now that we've discussed some of the barriers that might get in the way of us finding our people, let's dig a little deeper into some of the messaging about making new friends and the mindset shifts that might help this process be more enjoyable. It takes a certain amount of self-trust when stepping out there to find new friends. Do you trust your own ability to evaluate a person who enters your life and know whether or not they are someone you want to get to know better? Do you know what you like; what draws you and what repels you? And if you don't currently trust yourself in this regard, how do you become more confident in your ability to choose relationships that will add value to your life?

Part of trusting yourself and gaining that confidence comes with knowing that you don't have to stay in any situation that doesn't feel the way you would like it to. Some of our inability to trust ourselves comes from thinking we can't say "no, this doesn't work for me." We often feel as though we are required to stick it out if it's not "that bad." We falsely believe that looking specifically for what we want is selfish somehow. Just like in our romantic relationships, though, every sister you meet is not *the one*. Don't go into a situation with a stranger and tell them all your business or do too much too soon. Take baby steps. If you are at a conference and you meet a sister who seems really cool, maybe the first step is exchanging IG handles. Then maybe stay connected through random DMs every now and then or send each other inspirational memes. Maybe the relationship stays in that realm— that's okay. Or maybe you are able to move forward to meeting: "Hey, do you want to grab lunch one day?" And so on. The goal is seeing how the person moves in different kinds of situations. Share a little bit and see what they are willing to share.

Being intentional about what you're looking for in terms of friendship can help guide your first steps on this path. Are you looking for more mom friends or friends to run with? Ideally, you'd want to start spending time in places where these people congregate. For mom friends, this might mean getting involved with a parent organization at your child's school or joining an online group for moms in your area. For running friends, search online for information about local running groups, or inquire through your local running store. Some running stores even facilitate meetups for area runners, so explore this option. Whatever the interest is, there are likely places where other people with this interest congregate, so find out where that is and then plan a few visits. And while it can help to be intentional about what you're looking for in terms of friendship, I also want you to remain open to the surprise and delight of a sister entering your life in a package you weren't even expecting. You never know what new interest you might pick up because you meet someone new and they share it with you.

AN APPROACH FOR EVERY SISTER

I honestly believe that one of the best places to find your people is online. I shared in the previous chapter my thoughts on what sisterhood can look like in digital spaces because I truly believe in its potential. I believe in it so strongly because there is literally a digital space for everything you could possibly be interested in, so it makes sense to take advantage of technology in this way. Now, of course, I have to start by telling you what we do over in the Therapy for Black Girls Sister Circle. I describe it as our cozy corner of the internet designed just for Black women. It's a great space to be in if you're looking for a place to connect with sisters across the world. We have conversations about all kinds of things like mental health, personal development, pop culture, haircare, and travel. We also have weekly events designed for sisters to unwind, learn, and play together. We'd love to have you and you can join us at community.therapyforblackgirls.com.

If you're an app person, there are a few apps that have been created to help women connect to other women with like interests. Some women I know have found great success with Bumble BFF, and I've also heard good things about Hey! VINA. I know apps can be a bit scary and they're not for everyone, but, no worries, there are lots of other options.

Though not expressly for finding friends, Twitter and Instagram can also be good spaces to find sisters with similar interests. One of the best ways to start finding your people on these platforms is by following hashtags that are likely to take you to spaces and posts where Black women congregate. Some that may be of interest include #BlackGirlMagic, #CiteBlackWomen, #BlackBookstagram, #BuyFromABlackWoman, and #BlackGirlsRun. Following and searching these hashtags should lead you to lots of different pages of individual sisters whom you can engage with by reading or looking at what they post. Included in these hashtags will also be events, both virtual and IRL, that may be of interest to you and serve as an additional way of connecting with new sisters.

The digital spaces where I've seen Black women have the most success with finding their people are Facebook groups. For better or worse, Facebook makes it incredibly easy for you to find groups designed just for Black women about almost any topic. Do you love gardening? Black Girls Garden has a community of sisters just waiting for you to join them. Just bought your Peloton and want to find your people? Black Girl Magic: The Peloton Edition is a wonderful place to find Black women spinners at various levels of their workout journey. If you love a good DIY project, then the Black Girls Craft group just might be for you. If you're interested in looking for other groups, simply open the search bar in the Facebook app or on the home page and type in an interest; you can then filter for groups and learn more about them.

Similar to engagement in real life, when participating in an online space, it's a good idea to release the expectation that you'll be able to find your new best friend. A common interest means these spaces are ripe for actually making friends without the pressure; that's why I encourage you to join them. But those friendships will still likely only happen organically. Even in a group of more than thirty thousand Black women like Black Girl Magic Peloton, you might notice that you and another sister who regularly engage have the same favorite instructor. You might note that every time you see her comments you end up laughing or smiling. Follow that joy. Maybe add her as a friend or follow her personal page. There shouldn't be any pressure for her to be your person, but you can still take the opportunity to grow your engagement with her. Online groups and digital spaces give you a really good way to learn something about other sisters from a distance. If you're Gen X or older, you might be thinking, "All that online stuff is cute, Dr. Joy, but it's not for me." Not a problem. I've got some ideas for you too. Is there a sister whom you see frequently when you drop your little one off at school? What about the sister who always sits next to you in yoga? What would it be like for you to go up to her and introduce yourself one day soon? How do you think it might go if you ask the sister if she'd like to grab a smoothie after yoga? Sometimes our new friends aren't that new at all. I believe that there are often sisters in our lives whom we could be closer to with just a little effort and courage. And, yes, this takes us back to that conversation about the fear of rejection, right? But what's the worst that can happen? You never know until you try. SHOOT YOUR SHOT!

Another option for finding new people is to be intentional about going to the places you enjoy even if it means going solo. Do the things you are interested in and there's a high probability that you'll meet other people in those spaces with whom you have at least one thing in common. Sign up for that photography class you've been thinking about, grab your tickets for the walking history tour you saw advertised last week, look more into the Black ski trip that's being held next winter. Whatever you're interested in, you can trust that others are too and that you'll have a good time because it's something you genuinely want to do.

After you successfully shoot your shot and Sis says she'd love to grab lunch, I want you to work hard at showing up to the lunch as the most you version of you possible. This is your opportunity to show up as authentically as you can in hopes that you can truly connect with someone with a like mind. Be confident in the knowledge that who you are, where you've been, and what you desire is enough. I mean, sure, rock your cute outfit. You know we love a good slay. But be yourself because that's the person you want this sister to meet and get to know. Feel comfortable asking the questions you really want answers to. Where do they come from? What kind of work do they do? And in all of that, keep your expectations realistic. A fun lunch might not mean that this sister is a candidate for your close sister circle. At least, not yet. Be open and kind but also pay attention to any pink or red flags that pop up. Does the person seem like they're looking for the same thing as you? As you are asking questions about them, are they asking questions about you? Be attuned to it. And guess what? Whether they end up in your wedding or you never run into them again, being open to finding friendships and meeting new people—the very act of that—is healing all by itself. You did it! You knew that there might be judgment. You knew that rejection was possible, and yet you went for it anyway. If it does not go anywhere past that first lunch, be gentle with yourself and try not to pick yourself apart.

During our conversation Dr. Franco also shared that a rejection of a new friendship rarely has to do with anything about us personally; it is most often about whether that person feels like they can meet our needs. It is about whether they believe the effort required to get the friendship off the ground will be low enough to be worth it. If they decide that it is not, that is more about them than it is about us. Don't let one rejection take you out of the game permanently.

Organizations and Events of Interest

Getting involved with organizations or attending events that champion causes that are important to us or that cater to interests we enjoy is another great way to find like-minded sisters. Many of them may offer both virtual and IRL opportunities for getting involved and connecting, so you're bound to find something that allows you to engage with others. An easy way to find options in your area is by scrolling through Eventbrite. There you will see events happening in your area but you can also look for events across the country. Using the search function on either Instagram or TikTok can also be a great way to find events in your area or organizations committed to the kinds of things you're interested in. Finally, don't forget to look at the calendar of events for your local colleges and universities. Campuses often invite notable figures to give lectures or performances that are open to the public, and you might also be able to find a variety of continuing education opportunities connected to your interests.

The process of putting ourselves out there to meet new people isn't always easy, but it's courageous and important. I've had the amazing opportunity to witness the many ways in which community exists for sisters. From city meetups to "mommy groups," to church groups and volunteer opportunities, to digital spaces for Black women who love to build furniture or decorate planners. There is literally a community of Black women for every sister. Find yours!

QUESTIONS FOR REFLECTION

1. Where did you meet the last sister who became one of your people? When did you know that she was going to be someone important to you?

2. If you struggle with making new friends, what are some of the barriers getting in your way?

3. Are you open to the idea of new friends at this point in your life? Even if you are not looking, how might you respond to someone in your orbit who is perhaps looking to increase their circle?

The Charge:
Where Do We Go from Here?

Okay, ladies, now let's get in formation.

—Beyoncé

It has often felt frivolous to write about sisterhood while the world around me seemingly crumbles. I've questioned whether there's something different I could be offering my community, wondering if this will be enough. But then I get reminders, usually through the words of one of you, that this is indeed what is needed. There will most assuredly be tons of work to do, and who even knows what the world will look like when you're reading this. But I do know that all of that work will require us to have a strong foundation built on mutual respect, trust, and the pooling of as many resources as we can muster. I recently read a tweet from Creative Director Duanecia Clark in which she stated that she had been looking into resources to help her understand what might be needed in this moment in history and what might see us through. She shared that it was the Spanish flu pandemic of 1918 that preceded the birth of the Harlem Renaissance in 1920. Our people created, envisioned, and freely shared their gifts to get through that period, and we've seen some of this too. The balm that was seasons 4 and 5 of *Insecure, Black Panther: Wakanda Forever,* and Beyoncé's *Renaissance* album all come to mind.

If a client came to me with a similar question of "Is this enough?" I would remind them that we all have our own work to do in making things better. No one's work is better than or less than. All of it is important, and there's a reason you've been called to do this work at this time. Pay attention and stay open to the why. I submit that this was my work to complete at this time, an offering that will perhaps help us to make it to the other side a little more connected. But I can't do it alone. We have to do it together.

Will you join me in revising the stories we tell ourselves about one another? Will you join me in being a little kinder and gentler with yourself so that you can also offer the same to a sister? In being a little slower with judgment and a little quicker with curiosity about how something came to be? Will you join me in looking around to see if there is a sister feeling left out and being intentional to include her? In celebrating a sister's moment in the spotlight and then accepting the praise when it's your turn to be celebrated? Individually, these may seem to be small asks, and in some ways they are, but how different will our worlds look in three, five, or ten years if we put these things into practice? How might we all feel about ourselves and one another if these things are a reality?

I hope that what you've found here are some steps to get you started in that process. I hope that you're walking away as we end our time together here with a deeper connection to the joy that is found when we gather and a clearer understanding of why that happens. I hope you feel armed with skills to help you navigate the conflicts that will undoubtedly come up in your sister circles and feel more confident in how you can engage with other sisters online. I hope that you feel better prepared to be a soft place for a sister to land and that, if necessary, you're leaving feeling a little more comfortable at landing. I hope that you're leaving feeling a little more confident in our ability to create a world where sisters can believe it when we say "we got you."

———

GOODBYE

I've spent a lot of time talking about why goodbyes are important, so it wouldn't feel right if I didn't share one with you after the time you've spent with me here. While I've been writing, I've been reading certain passages aloud and imagining how you'll respond. Ha! Do you do that too? I've been wondering which topics we'll have the juiciest conversations about. I can't wait to dig into this with you. Even though I may not have met you yet, I feel like I know you. The process of writing this book has made that even clearer for me. So many times, I've become emotional as I crafted these paragraphs because the specialness of our story and our bonds is so precious and sacred to me. I hope I've done it justice on the page. As this process winds down, it feels like all of this has come full circle. I began the book by talking about the unspoken rules of sisterhood and as I close they feel very present for me. Writing this book and doing the work of Therapy for Black Girls with and for you has allowed me to be seen and for me to see you. You have supported me while I created spaces to support you, and I have gained a greater knowledge of myself. I think you will too. We have created together a soft place for all of us to land. Thank you for taking this journey with me. I deeply appreciate you.

Sister Acts:
A Resource for Ways We Can Engage Our Sisters

There is no one-size-fits-all model for "how to be a good sister," but I do think there are some things that we can do to start. I've created a list below that includes actions you can take both in your personal circle of sisterfriends and within the global sisterhood to become more intentional in creating the world we'd like to see. The list is not at all meant to be exhaustive, and I would love for you to add to it with Sister Acts of your own.

PERSONAL RELATIONSHIPS

Snail mail still works.

I love a good group chat as much as the next sister, but there's still something really special about getting physical mail delivered. Write a quick letter catching her up on life or grab a beautiful postcard to let her know you're thinking of her. You could also put together a care package of goodies you know she'll love and drop it in the mail.

Pick her up from the airport.

I know it's common to just grab an Uber from the airport, but if you can, picking a sister up from the airport when she returns from a trip can be a great way to get some unexpected time together. It's also one of those favors people hate asking for, so volunteering for the task is often a welcome gesture.

Lighten her load.

If a friend is not feeling well or recently became a mama, help her out by sending over a meal or by scheduling a grocery delivery. You can even cook and freeze some extra servings of meals you've prepared to stock up her fridge. This is also a great way to get the rest of the sister circle involved as you can all take turns sending over food or groceries.

Send her some flowers.

A fresh delivery of a beautiful arrangement brings a smile to anyone's face. If she just crushed an accomplishment, has been feeling down, or even just because, random flowers being delivered can be a nice pick-me-up. Pro tip: To keep costs down, consider grabbing a bundle from your local Trader Joe's or grocery store and drop them off on her doorstep or at her office.

Check in on your grieving friends.

Soon after the death of a loved one there is lots of activity, lots of people checking in, bringing food, etc. But after about a month the flurry dissipates, and this is often when our grieving sisters need us most. Set reminders in your calendar to check in at the six-week mark, again at the three-month mark, and again at the six-month mark. It can also help to add a note to your calendar for the eleven-month mark to remind you that she may begin to need some extra love and care as the one-year anniversary approaches. Don't fret about what to say or what to do, just let her know you're there.

Give her a break.

Offer to babysit for your sisters who are mamas. Every mother needs a chance to get away, either with her partner or alone to replenish and restore. Maybe she needs some emergency help for a last-minute work situation, or maybe she'd just like to eat her dinner without little hands dipping in her mashed potatoes. Whatever the situation, offer to give her a break if you can, and if possible don't wait for her to ask. We know mamas often struggle with mommy guilt and feel like they're being selfish for asking for help. Beat her to it.

Cash App your girl.

A random "coffee on me" Venmo or Cash App gift is always a wonderful surprise and sends the message that you're thinking of her. It could also be a gentle reminder for her to do something nice for herself that day.

Send her a playlist.

Music is healing, relaxing, and empowering. Send your Sis one of the new favorites you've found or compile one of your own that reminds you of her. She'll have a blast dancing and singing along to something that was inspired by her.

Support her self-care.

Listen, if you scratch my scalp, I'm going to be your bestie forever. Self-care is best when it's consistent and intentional. Supporting and uplifting your sister in self-care practices could look like painting her nails, giving her a pedicure, taking a walk to get some fresh air, scratching or massaging her scalp, or just allowing space for a long, loving hug.

Buy a book (maybe this one?).

If you and your girls are avid readers, what better way to share joy with the sister you love than buying her a book or sending her an audiobook? It can be a thoughtful reminder for her to take some time to relax, read, and be encouraged, especially if you choose a book she's been wanting or one on a topic she's been talking about. Pro tip: If time allows, arrange for an informal book club where the entire circle reads the same book and gets together on a Saturday with snacks to discuss.

Send a funny meme in the group chat.

Sending a funny (or scandalous, thought-provoking, or inspiring) meme or GIF to your friends is a good way to check in with someone or communicate when all of you are busy and don't have much time to chat that day or week. They can be good pick-me-ups and can serve as low-energy signs of life.

Plan a girls' trip.

Whether that's getting a hotel room with friends in your city and vegging out on popcorn and sweet tea, or hitting up Essence Fest with a "whatever happens there, stays there" pact, spending time with your sisterfriends can strengthen bonds and mend fences, if needed.

Celebrate friendiversaries.

Celebrating anniversaries and milestones is an important cultural tradition. A friendiversary is a fun reminder of all the wonderful moments and memories shared. It's a nice way to maintain appreciation and joy in your friendship.

Invite your work sister out.

You already have something in common and you might be able to grow your circle by simply inviting your sister acquaintance from work to your church, mosque, favorite club, gym, or restaurant. I mean, whatever your thing is, ask homegirl to join you for it.

Leave her a Post-it note.

Do you need a creative and inconspicuous way to encourage a sisterfriend? Post-it notes on her desk could be a thoughtful way to positively affirm, uplift, and encourage her at work. Leave a sweet reminder that she is seen.

Back her up in meetings.

If you are in a meeting, make sure that your sister's voice is heard. Defy the "there can only be one" systems and instead of participating in an echo chamber of the same ol' voices, be a part of creating a safe space for reassurance and validation. This is especially important if you are in a leadership position.

Make a gift basket or goodie bag for the new sister in the office.

We all know what it can be like to be the new girl in the office. Make it a little easier for the next sister by prepping a small goodie bag for her with some office supplies, a nice journal, and maybe a gift card to your favorite local lunch spot.

Help a sister stunt in an interview.

Interviews can be nerve-racking and many of us have a tendency to sell ourselves short. If a sister is interviewing for a position and you have the opportunity to ask a question as part of a panel, ask something that will allow her to brag on herself and display why she'd be a good fit.

Make sure elderly sisters in your neighborhood are taken care of.

Offer to run errands or stop by frequently just to check in. At the change of seasons make sure they have a safe way to heat and cool their homes or have access to heating and cooling centers.

Fly or drive in to see your girl as a surprise.

Who doesn't love a good surprise? (Well, actually, some people don't, so only try this one if you know she'd enjoy it.) Yes, planned visits are important, but if you can manage to sneak into town without her knowing, that will be a visit neither of you will forget.

Make a big deal out of birthdays, even if she doesn't.

Now listen, if your sisterfriend is someone who doesn't enjoy a spectacle, please don't throw her a surprise black-tie party for her fortieth birthday. Some people genuinely do not like all the extra razzle-dazzle, but I still think it's important to let people know they are seen, loved, and considered on their birthdays, even if it's just an ice cream cake and a new pair of fuzzy socks. Make the effort.

Help her find a therapist.

Sometimes people know they need support but get overwhelmed by the process. Use the Therapy for Black Girls therapist directory at therapyforblackgirls.com to help a sister find a therapist who might be a good fit for her. You can do an initial search and then share three to five names of therapists for her to choose from.

Schedule an adult field day.

As we get older, we often lose our sense of play, but being playful is important throughout our lives, not just as kids. Help your circle re-engage their sense of play by planning an adult field day complete with a potato sack race and a Hula-Hoop contest. If that's not quite your speed, consider a backyard movie night or game night complete with everyone's favorite snacks.

Move her in for a few days.

If there's a sister in your circle who's had a recent breakup, drive on over to her home and help her pack a week's worth of clothes and whatever else she needs to stay with you.

The immediate aftermath of a breakup can be brutal and getting her out of her typical surroundings can provide an important reset.

———

THE GLOBAL SISTERHOOD

Grab a pack of "I see you" cards to share.

I know I'm not the only one who loved getting and giving those cute little Valentine cards in grade school. I want to bring that energy back with cards to share with sisters as we see one another out in the world. I've already discussed the power of being seen by other sisters and sharing quick notes with one another is a way to make that tangible.

Send a sister a drink or a dessert.

If you are in a restaurant and you see a sister dining alone, send over a drink or a nice dessert while asking the server to relay a kind, affirming message.

If a sister is dining alone, ask if she'd like to join you.

I know this one seems chancy, but you also never know what might happen. If you see a sister dining alone and you're dining alone but would be down for some company, ask if she'd like to join you. At the very least, you both have a great meal and conversation, but this random encounter could also turn out to be an incredible connection.

Offer to help.

If you notice that a sister is upset, approach her kindly and ask her if there is anything you can do to help or if she needs anything at that moment, even if it's just a hug.

Be ready to step up.

If you see a sister in public who looks uncomfortable in a situation and you are able to intervene safely, say something like "Hey, girl, are you ready to roll?" or "Excuse me, that's a beautiful bag—where'd you get it?" or anything random that would distract the other party and give her an opportunity to exit.

Connect with the custodial and janitorial staff.

Be intentional about engaging with sisters who are service workers. They are oftentimes overlooked and undervalued. If there are sisters in your workspace that you see often, offer to have lunch with them or buy them lunch. And don't forget about them during the holidays: A nice gift card or some homemade goodies are thoughtful ways to share your appreciation.

Share your favorite products and services from a Black woman-owned business.

If there's a product or service you use and love, tell everybody you know. Drop it in the group chat, share it on your social media channels, and leave a stellar review.

Hype them up.

"Yaaasss, hair!" "Girl, you look amazing!" Black women have this on lock. It's our superpower. Compliments are known to uplift the giver and the receiver. Practice giving verbal compliments daily to your sisters, and don't forget our little sisters.

Pay for groceries or Starbucks or a meal for a sister.

When you are out and about, if there's a sister behind you in the line surprise her by paying for her groceries or coffee. If you are in a drive-through and see a sister in the rearview, you could pay for her meal. Pay it Black-ward!

Send a note of thanks.

Have you recently read an article, a book, or an academic paper written by a sister that was particularly impactful or that you really enjoyed? Let her know. Send a quick email, Tweet, or DM telling her that you read it and enjoyed it and a quick note about why. Writing can be a pretty solitary activity, and letting someone know that their work impacted you can be just the boost they need to get through that next assignment.

Start or donate to a community fridge.

Put together a team of sisters and work to start or support a community fridge to help expand access to food options. If you're a couponer, this is a great way to put those skills to use to help others with your next big haul.

Volunteer to tutor or teach a class with a local youth organization.

Supporting our little sisters is a great way to keep the sisterhood moving forward. Volunteer to help with homework or teach them a skill that you enjoy.

Support the WNBA.

These women are incredible and don't get nearly enough shine. Attend a game if you can but if not stream them online. You can also support them by grabbing some merch.

Share your medical providers.

It can be hard to find good medical care. If you've found some great healthcare providers, share the names with other sisters who may be looking.

Ask for the manager.

When you receive excellent customer service from a sister in a restaurant or store, tell or leave a note for the manager.

Mentor younger sisters in your profession.

There are more people watching you than you know. Younger sisters are often interested in learning how we've gotten to where we are professionally, so make it easy for them to find out. If you don't have the bandwidth to do any one-on-one mentoring, hold a virtual call twice a year where students and young professionals in your area can learn about what you do and you can share any helpful resources.

Sponsor a book scholarship for a sister at your alma mater.

Every year textbooks get more and more expensive. Consider starting a book scholarship for a sister (or several if you can swing it) at your alma mater or an HBCU to help with the costs of completing her education.

Support your local shelters.

If you have gently used clothing you can donate to those in need, please do so. Many shelters also accept other hard-to-get items like toiletries, diapers, and formula. If you can donate some items or make a financial donation to support the work of the shelter, please do.

Donate your time to help a sister find work.

If you're good at crafting or reviewing résumés, donate your time to a local organization to help with résumé reviews or mock interviews for sisters who may be looking for employment.

Acknowledgments

This book would not have been possible without the countless brilliant Black women writers who made it okay to center and marvel in a world by and for Black women. Thank you for your scholarship and the love and care with which you have laid a foundation for many to follow. I am grateful for you.

To my husband, Dennison, for making me laugh when this process got tough, for making sure I was fed and that my babies were well tended to while I poured myself into writing. I could not have done this without your support. I love you. Thank you.

To my babies, Jackson and Julian, for making sure I remembered to still have fun and for checking on me to see how the writing was going. Thank you for being patient with this process. I love you.

To my parents, Pat and Robert, for supporting each and every single dream I've ever had. Thank you for helping me to believe the sky was the limit and for being along for the ride. I'm grateful for all of your love and sacrifices.

To my brothers, Todd and Chad, for the endless laughs, constant encouragement, and support. I'm a very proud big sister.

To my aunties and cousins for being my very first examples of sisterhood. Our time together on the porch has meant more to me than you'll ever know. It is where this all started and I am grateful for your years of love, laughter, and support.

To the circle of sisters who have loved and held me through various parts of my life, I am so grateful to you. Tanya, Nicole, Nafeesa, Nikkii, Anastasia, Melanie, Key, Ayanna, and Joy, you make life so much sweeter. Thank you for everything.

To my agent Rebecca for recognizing I had a message to share in a book long before I did. Thank you for supporting my vision and helping me to get clear about what I wanted to say and how I wanted to say it. I am grateful for your care and diligence.

To my editor Chelcee for believing in this work and recognizing the importance of it. Thank you for your support and guidance through this process and for helping me to shape this into a book I'm very proud of.

Thank you to the teams at Ballantine and Random House for your excitement and enthusiasm about the book and for all of your hard work in making it possible.

Alisha, thank you for helping me to get clear about the focus of the book and the message I wanted to convey. I am grateful for our time spent brainstorming and reveling in the world of sisterhood.

Tracey, you describe yourself as a book doula and there could not be a better term for how you helped me bring this book to life. Thank you for the countless conversations and for embodying the spirit of this project. Thank you for letting me borrow your faith when things felt tough and for guiding me across the finish line. I am grateful for all your work in helping my words to sing on the page and for the relationship we cultivated in the process.

To the incredible sisters who accompany me on the Therapy for Black Girls team, I am eternally grateful. Thank you for the care, creativity, and commitment you demonstrate to this work and to our community. I am so honored to have you on the team and grateful for your love and support in completing the book.

I am often amazed and amused that this is what I get to do for work. I am so incredibly grateful to the Therapy for Black Girls community for all the ways you support me, whether it be enjoying a podcast episode, sharing a word of support in the comments section, being listed in the therapist directory, or sharing the directory with others. I knew this work was important, but I never could have imagined the ways you all have shown up for yourself, one another, and me. I am grateful for each of you. A very special thank you to the members of the Sister Circle for your love and support. Your excitement about the book has been such a balm. Thank you!

Notes

INTRODUCTION

1. Patricia Hill Collins, *Black Feminist Thought: Knowledge, Consciousness, and the Politics of Empowerment* (New York: Routledge, 2002).

2. From an interview Shange did with Claudia Tate in the book *Black Women Writers at Work* (Chicago: Haymarket Books, 2023).

3. Rashad's talk at the Enterprise Women of Power Summit, March 6, 2020, in Las Vegas, Nevada.

4. Katrina Bell McDonald, *Embracing Sisterhood: Class, Identity, and Contemporary Black Women* (Lanham, Md.: Rowman & Littlefield, 2007).

5. Nicole Knickmeyer MS, Kim Sexton MS, and Nancy Nishimura EdD, "The Impact of Same-Sex Friendships on the Well-Being of Women," *Women & Therapy* 25, no. 1 (2002): 37–59, https://doi.org/10.1300/J015v25n01_03.

6. Angel Nduka-Nwosu, "Black Sisterhood in Music," *AMAKA Studio,* June 21, 2022, https://amaka.studio/explore/articles/black-sisterhood-in-music.

7. bell hooks, *All About Love: New Visions* (New York: William Morrow, 2000), 215.

CHAPTER 1:
WHAT SHAPES OUR CONNECTIONS

1. R.I.M. Dunbar, "The Anatomy of Friendship," *Trends in Cognitive Sciences* 22, no. 1 (2018): 32–51, https://doi.org/10.1016/j.tics.2017.10.004.

2. J. Holt-Lunstad, T. B. Smith, and J. B. Layton, "Social Relationships and Mortality Risk: A Meta-Analytic Review," *PLOS Medicine* 7, no. 7 (2010): e1000316, https://doi.org/10.1371/journal.pmed.1000316.

3. Harvard Health Publishing, "The Health Benefits of Strong Relationships," December 1, 2010 https://www.health.harvard.edu/staying-healthy/the-health-benefits-of-strong-relationships.

4. Paul S. Greenman and Susan M. Johnson, "Emotionally Focused Therapy: Attachment, Connection, and Health," *Current Opinion in Psychology* 43 (2022): 146–50, https://doi.org/10.1016/j.copsyc.2021.06.015.

5. Nikki Giovanni, *Gemini* (New York: Penguin, 1971).

6. Geoffrey L. Greif and Tanya L. Sharpe, "The Friendships of Women: Are There Differences Between African Americans and Whites?," *Journal of Human Behavior in the Social Environment* 20, no. 6 (2010): 791–807, https://doi.org/10.1080/10911351003751892.

7. J. A. Abrams, A. Hill, and M. Maxwell, "Underneath the Mask of the Strong Black Woman Schema: Disentangling Influences of Strength and Self-Silencing on Depressive Symptoms Among U.S. Black Women," *Sex Roles* 80, no. 9/10 (2019): 517–26, https://doi.org/10.1007/s11199-018-0956-y.

8. LaToya Hampton, "Generations of Pain: A Transgenerational Examination of Trauma, Parenting Styles, and Attachment of Black Women," *Dissertations* 623 (2021): 64, https://digitalcommons.nl.edu/diss/623.

9. R. A. Dansby Olufowote, S. T. Fife, C. Schleiden, and J. B. Whiting, "How Can I Become More Secure?: A Grounded Theory of Earning Secure Attachment," *Journal of Marital and Family Therapy* 46 (2020): 489–506, https://doi.org/10.1111/jmft.12409.

10. M. Mikulincer and P. R. Shaver, *Attachment Patterns in Adulthood: Structure, Dynamics, and Change* (New York: Guilford Press, 2007).

CHAPTER 2:
THE WHOLE IS GREATER THAN THE SUM OF ITS PARTS

1. I. D. Yalom and M. Leszcz, *The Theory and Practice of Group Psychotherapy*, 6th ed. (New York: Basic Books, 2020).

2. J. B. Miller and I. P. Stiver, *The Healing Connection: How Women Form Relationships in Therapy and Life* (Boston: Beacon Press, 1997).

3. J. Berzoff, "The Therapeutic Value of Women's Adult Friendships," *Smith College Studies in Social Work* 59, no. 3 (1989): 267–79, https://doi.org/10.1080/00377318909517358.

4. bell hooks, *Yearning: Race, Gender, and Cultural Politics* (Boston: South End Press, 1990).

5. J. D. Frank, E. Ascher, J. B. Margolin, H. Nash, A. R. Stone, and E. J. Varon, "Behavioral Patterns in Early Meetings of Therapeutic Groups," *American Journal of Psychiatry* 108, no. 10 (1952): 771–78, https://doi.org/10.1176/ajp.108.10.771.

6. Yalom and Leszcz, *Theory and Practice of Group Psychotherapy*.

CHAPTER 3:
I AM MY SISTER'S KEEPER AND SHE IS MINE

1. C. McCallum, "Giving Back to the Community: How African Americans Envision Utilizing Their PhD," *Journal of Negro Education* 86, no. 2 (2017): 138–53, https://doi.org/10.7709/jnegroeducation.86.2.0138.

2. N. M. Brown and R. Mendenhall, "Communal Conversations: Black Women World-Making Through Mentorship," *Qualitative Inquiry* (2022), https://journals.sagepub.com/doi/10.1177/10778004221124015.

3. Ariane Hegewisch and Eve Mefferd, "Lost Jobs, Stalled Progress: The Impact of the 'She-Cession' on Equal Pay," IWPR #C505 (September 2021), https://iwpr.org/wp-content/uploads/2021/09/Gender-Wage-Gap-in-2020-Fact-Sheet_FINAL.pdf.

224 Notes

4. Violence Policy Center, "When Men Murder Women: An Analysis of 2020 Homicide Data," September 2022, https://www.vpc.org/studies/wmmw2022.pdf.

5. Patricia Hill Collins, *Black Feminist Thought: Knowledge, Consciousness, and the Politics of Empowerment* (New York: Routledge, 2002), 104.

6. Audre Lorde, "The Master's Tools Will Never Dismantle the Master's House." 1984. *Sister Outsider: Essays and Speeches* (California: Crossing Press, 2007), p. 110–14.

CHAPTER 4:
THE LOAD IS LIGHTER WHEN WE HELP ONE ANOTHER CARRY IT

1. K.Y.-H. Liao, M. Wei, and M. Yin, "The Misunderstood Schema of the Strong Black Woman: Exploring Its Mental Health Consequences and Coping Responses Among African American Women," *Psychology of Women Quarterly* 44, no. 1 (2020): 84–104, https://doi.org/10.1177/0361684319883198.

2. D. C. Jack and D. Dill, "The Silencing the Self Scale: Schemas of Intimacy Associated with Depression in Women," *Psychology of Women Quarterly* 16, no. 1 (1992): 97–106, https://doi.org/10.1111/j.1471-6402.1992.tb00242.x.

3. J. A. Abrams, A. Hill, and M. Maxwell, "Underneath the Mask of the Strong Black Woman Schema: Disentangling Influences of Strength and Self-Silencing on Depressive Symptoms Among U.S. Black Women," *Sex Roles* 80, no. 9/10 (2019): 517–26, https://doi.org/10.1007/s11199-018-0956-y.

4. Abrams, Hill, and Maxwell, "Underneath the Mask of the Strong Black Woman Schema."

CHAPTER 5:
THERE IS SPACE FOR EVERYONE IN THE CIRCLE

1. Elisha Beach, "No One Champions a Black Woman Like Another Black Woman," *Scary Mommy,* February 12, 2021, https://www.scarymommy.com/importance-sisterhood-black-women/.

2. Thema Bryant-Davis, "Sister Friends: A Reflection and Analysis of the Therapeutic Role of Sisterhood in African American Women's Lives," *Women & Therapy* 36, no. 1/2 (2013): 110–20, https://doi .org/10.1080/02703149.2012.720906.

CHAPTER 8:
THE LIFE STAGES OF OUR CIRCLES

1. Kait Hanson, "Viral Post Shows What Friendship After Miscarriage Looks Like," *Today,* October 25, 2021, https://www .today.com/parents/miscarriage-friendship-post-goes-viral-t235916.

CHAPTER 9:
QUITE POSSIBLY THE WORST HEARTBREAK

1. Royette T. Dubar, "'Ghosting' Hurts: It May Have Psychological Consequences," *Washington Post,* July 26, 2022, https://www .washingtonpost.com/health/2022/07/25/ghosting-college-mental -health/.

2. Elisabeth Kübler-Ross, *On Death and Dying* (New York: Collier Books/Macmillan, 1970).

3. M. Stroebe and H. Schut, "The Dual Process Model of Coping with Bereavement: Rationale and Description," *Death Studies* 23, no. 3 (1999): 197–224, https://doi.org/10.1080/074811899201046.

4. D. L. Harris, "Non-Death Loss and Grief: Laying the Foundation," in *Non-Death Loss and Grief: Context and Clinical Implications* (New York: Routledge, 2020), 7–16, https://doi.org/10.4324 /9780429446054-2.

CHAPTER 10:
SISTERHOOD IS MOST NEEDED
IN THE PLACES YOU WOULDN'T EXPECT IT

1. M. Lizzio-Wilson, B. M. Masser, M. J. Hornsey, and A. Iyer, "You're Making Us All Look Bad: Sexism Moderates Women's Experience of Collective Threat and Intra-Gender Hostility Toward Traditional and Non-traditional Female Subtypes," *Group Processes & Intergroup Relations* 24, no. 8 (2021): 1486–514, https://doi.org /10.1177/1368430220913610.

2. https://www.1619books.com.

3. Melba Newsome, "Chemist Lisa Jones Withdraws from UNC Faculty Search over Pulitzer-Winning Journalist's Tenure Denial," *Chemical & Engineering News,* June 7, 2021, https://cen.acs.org /education/Nikole-Hannah-Jones-tenure-dispute-causes-a-chemist -to-withdraw-from-UNC-faculty-search/99/web/2021/06.

4. Tia Sherèe Gaynor, "A Love Letter to Black Women in the Academy," *Inside Higher Ed,* December 16, 2022, https://www .insidehighered.com/advice/2022/12/16/letter-support-and -solidarity-black-women-academe-opinion.

5. S. Rasheem, Ali-Sha Alleman, Dawnsha Mushonga, Darlene Anderson, and Halaevalu F. Ofahengaue Vakalahi, "Mentor-Shape: Exploring the Mentoring Relationships of Black Women in Doctoral Programs," *Mentoring & Tutoring: Partnership in Learning* 26, no. 1 (2018): 50–69, https://doi.org/10.1080/13611267.2018 .1445443.

6. J. Knoll, H. Schramm, C. Schallhorn, and S. Wynistorf, "Good Guy vs. Bad Guy: The Influence of Parasocial Interactions with Media Characters on Brand Placement Effects," *International Journal of Advertising* 34, no. 5 (2015): 740–43, https://doi.org/10 .1080/02650487.2015.1009350; H. Kim, E. Ko, and J. Kim, "SNS Users' Para-Social Relationships with Celebrities: Social Media Effects on Purchase Intentions," *Journal of Global Scholars of Marketing Science* 25, no. 3 (2015): 279–94, https://doi.org/10 .1080/21639159.2015.1043690.

7. S. Chung and H. Cho, "Fostering Parasocial Relationships with Celebrities on Social Media: Implications for Celebrity Endorsement," *Psychology & Marketing* 34, no. 4 (2017): 481–95, https://doi.org/10.1002/mar.21001.

8. bell hooks, *All About Love: New Visions* (New York: William Morrow, 2000).

CHAPTER 11:
THE COMPLEXITIES AND POSSIBILITIES
OF DIGITAL SISTERHOOD

1. L. Eichenbaum and S. Orbach, *Between Women: Love, Envy, and Competition in Women's Friendships* (New York: Viking, 1988).

DR. JOY HARDEN BRADFORD is a licensed psychologist and the host of the award-winning mental health podcast *Therapy for Black Girls*. Her work focuses on making mental health topics and support more relevant and accessible for Black women. She received a bachelor's degree in psychology from Xavier University of Louisiana, a master's degree in vocational rehabilitation counseling from Arkansas State University, and a Ph.D. in counseling psychology from the University of Georgia. Her work has been featured in *Essence, Oprah Daily, The New York Times, HuffPost, Black Enterprise,* and *Women's Health.* Dr. Joy Harden Bradford lives in Atlanta, Georgia, with her husband and two sons.

hellodrjoy.com
therapyforblackgirls.com
Instagram, X, TikTok: @hellodrjoy
Facebook.com/hellodrjoy